Practical IT Service Management

A concise guide for busy executives

Second edition

Practical IT Service Management

A concise guide for busy executives

Second edition

THEJENDRA B.S

IT Governance Publishing

Every possible effort has been made to ensure that the information contained in this book is accurate at the time of going to press, and the publisher and the author cannot accept responsibility for any errors or omissions, however caused. Any opinions expressed in this book are those of the author, not the publisher. Websites identified are for reference only, not endorsement, and any website visits are at the reader's own risk. No responsibility for loss or damage occasioned to any person acting, or refraining from action, as a result of the material in this publication can be accepted by the publisher or the author.

All ITIL definitions in this book are taken from the official ITIL® Glossary. The full glossary is available online - links are provided in the appendix.

ITIL® is a Registered Trademark of AXELOS Limited.

IT Governance Publishing
IT Governance Limited
Unit 3, Clive Court
Bartholomew's Walk
Cambridgeshire Business Park
Ely, Cambridgeshire
CB7 4EA
United Kingdom

www.itgovernance.co.uk

First published in the United Kingdom in 2008 by IT Governance Publishing

ISBN 978-1-905356-39-3

Second edition published in 2014.

ISBN 978-1-84928-546-9

PREFACE

Practical IT Service Management is a concise guide to implementing a professional, technical service management structure in your organisation, based on the international best practice framework ITIL® (Information Technology Infrastructure Library®). This framework is globally the most widely accepted approach to technical service management, and is developed based on input from several public and private sector organisations. This book explains the fundamentals of the latest ITIL 2011 version and its implementation in an easy, self-study approach for all technical and business staff in your organisation. The entire book is written in a question and answer format for easy comprehension and speedy reading. Each chapter covers just one specific area of ITIL, and each topic is explained concisely, with very few answers extending beyond one page. Practical and real-life examples are used throughout. *Practical IT Service Management* is designed to be a stepping stone to the official books on ITIL published by the The Stationery Office (TSO).

Unless stated otherwise, the names of the companies and people mentioned in the examples in this book are fictitious. The names of actual companies and products mentioned are the trademarks of their respective organisations. I would like to thank Alan Calder and Vicki Utting for their immense help in preparing this book. Although this manuscript has been prepared with the utmost care, the author, publisher, editor, or any other party associated with this book, can accept no liability for any direct or indirect damages caused by following the advice given here. However, suggestions for improvement, errors or mistakes observed, corrections required and any other relevant information that could be incorporated in a future edition, will be gratefully received at *thejendra@yahoo.com or thejendrabs@gmail.com.*

Thejendra B.S
January 2014

ABOUT THE AUTHOR

Thejendra B.S is an IT Manager for a software development company in Bangalore, India. Starting work as a field engineer, he has more than 20 years' experience in a wide range of roles in IT areas. He has been involved in IT support, help desk, DRP-BCP, asset management and IT security, and has implemented numerous small to large IT projects worth millions of pounds. Thejendra has worked in India, Saudi Arabia, Dubai, Bahrain, Qatar and Australia. During his years in the IT world, he has dealt with countless flavours of customers, vendors, end-users and organisations of all sizes. His articles have also been published on reputed websites, such as geekleaders.com, drj.com, ezinearticles.com, cio.com, techrepublic.com, cnbc.com, sourcingmag.com and many ezines.

Thejendra can be contacted at thejendra@yahoo.com or thejendrabs@gmail.com. For further details of his books and articles, please visit his website *www.thejendra.com.*

CONTENTS

Contents

Contents

Contents

Contents

Contents

Contents

Contents

INTRODUCTION

'A business absolutely devoted to service will have only one worry about profits. They will be embarrassingly large.'

Henry Ford

What is this book about?

The advancement and ease of availability of new and useful technologies has enabled thousands of organisations, worldwide, to implement, and become heavily dependent on, technology for running their businesses. It is not possible to run any organisation, small or big, without the use of some computer or telecom-related technologies. With so much proliferation of hardware, software and networking equipment it is necessary to have specialised and dedicated technology support departments to look after them. Otherwise, companies can get into serious trouble. A professional, technology support department is as essential to any organisation as a qualified finance department or a senior management team. Although organisations are free to have their own proprietary flavours of technical support, suiting their needs, it is always better to adopt some international best practices, as they prevent organisations from reinventing the wheel.

This concise book explains how to implement one such international best practice, ITIL. ITIL is a Registered Trademark, and all its contents are owned by the Cabinet Office, under the HM Government. Earlier ownership was with OGC (Office of Government Commerce). The publications (books) continue to be Crown Copyright. In addition, the Cabinet Office has entered into a joint venture with Capita plc. to commercialise its accreditation and publishing services, including ITIL. The new name for this joint venture company is called AXELOS, and it will inherit the entire portfolio of best management practice products from the Cabinet Office. The joint venture is expected to become fully operational by the middle of 2014. The term Axelos comes from a Greek-French philosopher named Kostas Axelos, who united old and new with games and openness.

All the ITIL concepts can be freely adopted by anyone implementing IT Service Management (ITSM) within their organisation. Written in a condensed style, *Practical IT Service Management* explains how you can interpret and implement the ITIL concepts in an easy, self-help format.

Who should read this book?

This book is written for busy IT executives in any organisation. Most busy executives often don't have the time, patience, luxury or interest to read detailed, academically-oriented IT books, due to their never-ending workloads and competitive pressures. They need quick, practical information on a topic or concept that will help them in their workplace. This book fills the needs of such an audience and will be of use to:

- Technical managers
- Technical support specialists
- IT consultants
- Chief technical officers

- Chief information officers
- Business managers
- And even members of the Board of Directors.

CHAPTER 1: INTRODUCTION TO IT SERVICE MANAGEMENT

What is IT?

The term 'IT' is an abbreviation of Information Technology. A general dictionary defines IT as the development, installation and implementation of computer systems, telecommunications and software applications. In practical terms, IT consists of:

1. Computers, such as desktops, servers, laptops, mainframes, and the data that they hold.

2. Software, such as operating systems (Windows, Unix, Linux, Novell, specialised operating systems) and applications, such as word processors, spreadsheets, databases, productivity tools, business applications and custom-built applications.

3. Communication and telecom equipment, such as PBX, lease lines, the Internet, telephone networks, Local Area and Wide Area Networks.

4. Other specialised IT equipment and software.

The ITIL definition of IT is:

'The use of technology for the storage, communication or processing of information. The technology typically includes computers, telecommunications, applications and other software. The information may include business data, voice, images, video, etc. Information technology is often used to support business processes through IT services.'

What are IT services?

The term 'IT services' refers to a set of support and maintenance functions provided by technically qualified staff (internal or outsourced) to an organisation that uses various computers, software, printers, hardware and communication facilities. An IT service may range from providing access to a simple application, such as a word processor for all end-users, or access into a complex network consisting of hundreds of different types of computers, operating systems, servers, e-mail systems, websites, databases, telecom systems and Internet access used by hundreds of end-users inside an organisation.

The ITIL definition of an IT service is:

'A service provided by an IT service provider. An IT service is made up of a combination of information technology, people and processes. A customer-facing IT service directly supports the business processes of one or more customers and its service level targets should be defined in a service level agreement. Other IT services, called supporting services, are not directly used by the business but are required by the service provider to deliver customer-facing services.'

What is IT service management?

The term *IT Service Management* refers to an orderly and professional method followed by an IT department to provide reliable and efficient information systems and support to meet your business requirements. Most organisations now understand the benefits of having IT throughout their internal environment, but do not understand the need for managing it properly. If IT equipment and services are not managed correctly in your organisation, you could get into serious trouble. Firstly, and as mentioned earlier, no modern organisation can run its operations, or survive, without using one or more computers, software, telecommunications and the Internet. If an important computer system stops working, then business may have to stop if it is not possible to switch over to alternative manual processes for any length of time. Secondly, computer systems and networks are extremely complex and complicated for any business person to maintain, or support, on their own. Specialised employees are required who understand how those systems work and how to babysit them. IT services should be in alignment with your business strategy and objectives. From a simple nuts and bolts perspective, IT service management means that the 'techies' (employed or outsourced) in the organisation are professionally managing and maintaining the computers, networks, telecommunications, data storage and retrieval, e-mail systems and databases, owned or used by your business.

The ITIL definition of IT service management is:

'The implementation and management of quality IT services that meet the needs of the business. IT service management is performed by IT service providers through an appropriate mix of people, process and information technology.'

What problematic issues do IT departments commonly face?

Running an IT department is a herculean task. There will always be difficulties and headaches to keep the staff perpetually busy and hassled. Some of the common obstacles faced by IT departments of many small, and even large, organisations include the following:

- Roles and responsibilities of staff are not clearly defined or are non-existent. No structured customer support mechanism is in place. No help desk or service desk facilities.

- Business managers do not understand (or try to understand) the technical department's work and constraints, and technical people do not understand (or try to understand) business people's needs.

- A single IT person or an IT team that is too small are responsible for anything and everything related to IT. Excessive workloads and poor career growth prospects.

- Lack of clearly defined and simple processes. No service level agreements, vendor agreements and technical training.

- Frequent disagreements between business and IT departments for service and cost expectations.

- Business and technical staff not seeing eye to eye. Poor management buy-in, inadequate funding, culture issues and resistance to change.

- Businesses not understanding the essential requirements for using IT in their organisations (proper IT staffing, exponential hardware and software budgets, ongoing costs and frequent and necessary upgrades).

- Technical staff concentrating only on technical matters, and unable, or unwilling, to understand business needs.

- No proactive IT problem prevention methods. Only reactive support. Issues get solved after they occur, with no prevention mechanism in place.

- IT staff using outdated tools and equipment, resulting in the IT department being out of sync with modern business demands.

What issues do businesses face through heavy dependence on IT?

In the 1990s only very large organisations could afford to use computers. At that time, IT was not considered as being essential to run a business. This thinking is no longer applicable, and IT has proved its benefits, even in the smallest of organisations. However, using information technology is a catch-22 situation, as businesses have become excessively dependent on IT. You cannot live with IT, nor can you live without IT. With so much dependence on IT there will be associated risks and issues. To fully answer this question, it is first necessary to understand how IT normally gets implemented in an organisation. Many organisations can easily buy the necessary computers, software and telecommunications for running their businesses. However, the implementation of IT is often carried out without proper planning of any sort due to numerous reasons, such as a lack of appropriate knowledge.

There will be several IT-related issues that will cause minor to major irritations, or even bring an organisation to an abrupt halt. The following examples show how many organisations implement IT and the hair-raising issues they can face.

Example of poor IT implementation:

The owner of a small business may buy a single computer, initially for general use. After discovering the benefits of using a computer, he may immediately decide to buy 25 more for his staff.

Within a short time his business will be computerised, and very soon IT support headaches will enter the business. Using a computer may be easy, but maintaining a computer system is a complicated task. Users may suddenly experience crippling virus attacks, equipment failures, software licensing issues, data corruption, data loss, back-up issues and upgrade issues. They may not be in a position to support and maintain a computer network and its associated functions. Overnight, a smart purchasing assistant may undergo a crash course in computer maintenance, or buy a book on *Computer Maintenance*, and soon will be given responsibility for the technical support of the business, along with his or her other responsibilities. IT departments begin their life in this way in many organisations. However, this sort of approach will lead to major and uncontrollable issues later on.

Example of poor and inadequate IT support:

Let us take a simple example of how a single hard disk crash can cripple your organisation. A technician who lacks business sensitivity may view a computer hard disk crash as a simple issue, whereas it may be seen as a critical issue for the business owner since the entire business and financial data may be on the failed disk. To add to the misery, the disk was probably not being backed up regularly. On the other side of the coin, the business owner may have earlier refused to invest money on an essential device, such as a tape drive for data back-up. Both parties will blame each other. A typical interaction between the help desk and the business departments in many organisations can be like this:

Finance Department: 'Hello. Our finance server is not working. Can you fix it?'

Help desk: 'Which one?'

Finance Department: 'The one that we use in our department. It's a black system with a green keyboard.'

Help desk: 'I had a look at it, but the hard disk is dead and we will have to replace it. I will call the vendor and arrange for a replacement if possible.'

Finance Department: 'What about our data?'

Help desk: 'I'm afraid we can't recover the data. The disk is dead and we have not been backing up the data of that server, because nobody told us to. Finance did not approve the purchase of a tape drive for this machine.'

Finance Department: 'Oh no. We have our entire payroll, purchasing, billing, sales and other important financial data for the entire company on that machine. Five years of data!'

Help desk: 'Unfortunately there is nothing we can do. Please excuse me, I have to go and attend another call.'

A situation like that can cripple your organisation within hours.

Other common IT headaches

Other IT-related frequent pin pricks and shocks can be as follows:

- Your end-users don't know who to contact when their computers and other IT equipment fail.

- Your techies attend end-user calls if they can, when they can.

- Business managers do not understand why their IT infrastructure is always having disruptions of a similar nature.

- Monday morning chaos. All computer systems are down

for some reason. The IT department probably performed some maintenance activities over the weekend.

- Businesses cannot commit about their products and services to their external customers. (*See next example.*)

- Your end-users do not know if all IT services will be available for them every day to complete their activities.

- Viruses, crippling and lengthy IT shutdowns, are common.

- End-users always face a shortage of computers, disk space, data corruption and data loss.

- Business managers do not know why they need to shell out another bag of cash for some software the IT department needs.

Example of IT breakdown affecting business:

New Sales Manager: 'Folks, where are you going? That sales quote must be sent to the Abacus Company today or we lose that account.'

Sales Team: 'We are going home. All computers are down. We can't prepare the sales quote without a computer.'

New Sales Manager: 'Home? When will the IT department fix it?'

Sales Team: 'They said it may take a couple of days or more.'

New Sales Manager: 'What? We can't wait that long.'

Sales Team: 'We do here. Very often it can take three days to fix IT issues. Computer breakdowns are quite frequent here.'

> **New Sales Manager:** 'This isn't good enough. I have committed the pricing quote to the Abacus Company. If I don't send it today we may lose a £50,000 order.'

How can professional IT service management help?

The above examples show what could happen to your organisation without a professional and proactive IT service department. Without such a department, your organisation could face crippling and profit-threatening situations. However, if you have implemented professional IT service management practices, such harrowing situations are less likely to occur. Even if an important disk has crashed, with professional IT service management it should be able to be restored in a matter of hours.

Haphazard IT support directly, or indirectly, impacts your main business. For example, will external customers open an account in a bank that has frequent and lengthy computer breakdowns, virus attacks and shutdowns? Or if your entire manufacturing operation is computerised, and if there are frequent IT breakdowns, think about the losses, delay and its business impact. Considering the complexity and importance of today's computer systems, it is imperative to bring in some measurable and verifiable IT service standards so that your business managers understand, amongst others, the IT department's scope of work, the deliverables, the constraints, the limitations and budgetary needs. It is absolutely vital for both IT and business departments to understand that the quality of support, its availability, and the recoverability of your IT infrastructure, will directly influence the quality, profitability and respectability of your organisation.

This is where professional IT service management, or ITIL, can help because these are industry best practices that can safeguard your organisation. Otherwise, your organisation may follow some proprietary service processes and methodologies that may, or may not, save you and also not be transparent, documented, controlled, measurable, repeatable and portable. By implementing IT service management, your business owners can have the satisfaction and peace of mind of knowing that the IT infrastructure necessary for running your business is in safe hands.

However, implementing a best practice IT service management system does not mean discarding every current process or method used by your organisation and starting from scratch. You can gradually implement an IT service management system that will be much more efficient than a method developed in-house.

CHAPTER 2: OVERVIEW OF ITIL 2011

'Call them rules or call them limits, good ones, I believe, have this in common: They serve reasonable purposes; they are practical and within a child's capability; they are consistent; and they are an expression of loving concern.'

Fred Rogers

This chapter provides an overview of ITIL 2011, which is the latest update released. Earlier versions will also be explained briefly, but elaborate comparisons will not be made between them, to avoid confusion. As mentioned earlier, ITIL is under copyright. No exact material, diagrams or contents from the official ITIL books are reproduced in this book, however, the exact ITIL definitions from the official ITIL glossary are mentioned in some chapters, just to elaborate the concepts being explained.

What is ITIL?

The term 'ITIL' refers to a best practice framework for IT service management, and consists of a series of official publications (books) giving exhaustive guidance on how to provide quality IT services in your organisation. The books explain the various processes and kinds of departments needed to support these IT services. As mentioned before, the best practice guidance contained in ITIL can be freely used by any organisation of any size, operating in any industry.

However, as soon as the word ITIL is mentioned, many overloaded and overburdened IT departments and business people start imagining all sorts of scary views, such as it is a bureaucratic process, it is very complex, it must be highly theoretical, which can only add to their woes, rather than reduce them. For IT managers involved in practical, technical aspects, the thick official ITIL books may seem like a detailed collection of dull processes, raising doubts on how they can actually use them in the real world. Also, many business people, IT departments and managements of small and medium organisations live in the misconception that ITIL is beyond their expertise or affordability, and perhaps applicable only to large organisations.

All the above fears are understandable because ITIL is created and maintained by a government organisation, unlike Six Sigma which was created by a Fortune 500 organisation, led by a glamorous CEO. After all, governments worldwide are known for their lethargic, obscure and bureaucratic processes that only delay and make things complex. However, as you can never judge a book by its cover, you should not judge ITIL by who created it. ITIL is not the scary stuff that most businesses imagine. Actually, ITIL is a lot of practical IT management common sense and not just some impractical theories. Generous doses of ITIL can be implemented by practically any organisation (small, medium or large) to bring some law and order to their IT infrastructure management. By implementing ITIL, you can avoid, or eliminate, various IT issues, and bring a very high degree of stability and predictability to your IT infrastructure. ITIL offers value and return on investment to every business owner, service provider, CIOs, CTOs and CEOs. However, extracting the wealth of advice given in ITIL actually depends on how you can *interpret* the given processes for practical purposes and apply them to your organisation. This book aims to help you achieve that *interpretation* in a short and realistic way.

Before you begin the actual journey of IT service management based on ITIL, it is necessary to understand the meaning of certain common words, such as **'business'**, **'customer'** and **'end-user'**, as used in the IT service management world. These are all core concepts of ITIL and hold good for all ITIL versions. This can be explained through an example.

Example: The RockSolid Corp:

Assume there is a modern company called RockSolid Corp, owned by Mr Johns, that manufactures and sells industrial air conditioners (a/c). The company has about a thousand employees spread among several departments, such as sales, finance, human resources, a/c engineering, clerical support, a/c technical design, support and a/c servicing. All these employees have been provided with a desktop computer, access to e-mail, telephones, the Internet, office applications and other software necessary for their departments. All are connected by Local and Wide Area Networks. There is also a separate department called the Technical Services Division, consisting of several employees (and also outsourced staff, such as technical contractors and consultants) trained and responsible for maintaining those computers, e-mail systems, Internet access software and networks. The Technical Services Division, in turn, has several sub-departments, or groups, specialising in a particular IT area, such as desktop support, network support, software support, service desk, data centre, IT strategy, planning and operations. All the departments of the Technical Services Division are located within the buildings of RockSolid Corp.

In addition, this Technical Services Division and its departments also have support and consultancy arrangements with various external vendors and specialists, ranging from common hardware and software suppliers, to ultra-specialist companies that can implement and maintain massive technical projects for the organisation. Such arrangements will be required because companies can no longer afford to employ all types of technical experts on their payroll. For example, RockSolid Corp may have a multimillion pound long-term contract with a massive telecommunications company (say ABC-Telecom) to meet and maintain all its telecom and networking needs on an end to end basis. In such cases, ABC-Telecom will be actively involved in some RockSolid Corp activities, such as decision making on technical upgrades, decommissioning obsolete equipment, providing support, maintaining infrastructure inventories, running telecom projects and providing account managers to route requests and generate reports. In such cases, ABC-Telecom can be called a 'technology partner' or an 'IT Service Provider' who will be dedicating a set of their employees to service RockSolid Corp.

As you may have observed, most large companies enter into long-term contracts with several IT service providers, to minimise having in-house expertise. A large bank or supermarket chain need not employ all types of technical specialists. Instead, they can hire, or enter into a long-term contract with, major IT service providers to meet all their needs.

According to ITIL, the following words have the following meanings.

- **Organisation**: means the RockSolid Corp, with all its employees, equipment, etc.

- **Business**: The primary business of RockSolid Corp is selling industrial air conditioners. Without selling air conditioners, the organisation cannot exist. As a rule, every air conditioner purchase order is processed and shipped within two business days.

- **IT services**: covers all the IT facilities and access to various applications, computers, telecommunications, software, databases, e-mail systems, web servers, associated infrastructure, and the Technical Services Division (with all its sub-departments) who look after that equipment in the RockSolid organisation. All the departments of the Technical Services Division are collectively, and collaboratively, responsible for maintaining the IT infrastructure of RockSolid Corp.

- **Customer**: This term has to be used carefully. A customer in ITIL is the person (or senior management) who pays for, and owns, the IT Services or the Technical Services Division. Typically, this is someone who is responsible for paying, or absorbing the cost of having an IT service within his or her organisation. In this case, the owner of RockSolid Corp, Mr Johns and his business managers, are the customers for IT services because they are paying money to own, or hire, the Technical Services Divisions. In turn, Mr Johns will have external customers who have purchased air conditioners manufactured by RockSolid Corp.

- **End-users**: The various employees and departments, such as sales, finance and HR within the RockSolid organisation who use the IT services on a day-to-day basis, are called end-users. They depend on IT services for running the business smoothly. The finance department will depend on IT services to maintain and support their payroll and accounts server. The engineering department will depend on IT services to maintain and support their design server. In many companies, end-user departments also pay, or get charged, for having regular or special services from IT services. End-users can also be treated as a flavour of customers of IT services from a broad perspective.

To summarise:

- Customers for IT services of RockSolid Corp are the business managers (who pay for having the IT services) and end-users who may directly, or indirectly, pay for these services. This book will deal mainly with these customers and look at how IT services provide effective internal support to the end-users, business managers and divisions inside the organisation(s). Whenever and wherever we mention the word customer in this book, it will always mean the employees and management of RockSolid Corp.

- Customers for RockSolid Corp are the various external companies and individuals who have purchased air conditioners. In this book we will not refer to these external customers.

What are the main benefits of using a framework, such as ITIL?

Many organisations believe they have already implemented excellent self-developed IT services and don't need to change, as the current framework might be acceptable to the business imperatives. However, on closer examination, these customised services will usually lack many necessary and essential processes that could enhance the IT department. The benefits of using professional IT service management processes, such as those in ITIL, are simply enormous:

- ITIL is a framework that offers benefits that demonstrate value and return on investment to every business owner, service provider, CIOs, CTOs and a CEO.

- Proven and tested processes. No need for businesses to reinvent the wheel for implementing IT services in their organisations. Covers end-to-end.

- Non-proprietary practices. Though ITIL is owned by HM Government, it does not require a license to practice, and it is independent of any commercial solution or platform. Every organisation can use the official ITIL books to implement the processes.

- Improved quality of IT service for business functions. Reduced downtime, improved customer and end-user satisfaction.

- Measurable, controllable, recoverable.

- ITIL is scalable. It can be adapted for any size of organisation.

- Proactive rather than reactive. Clearly defined roles, responsibilities and activities.

- Greater understanding of IT and its limitations. Business will understand IT better and vice versa.

- There are a range of accredited ITL training and education courses. This has resulted in the growth of a number of support services, training institutes, tools and consultancy services that can help your organisation's IT departments.

- Return on Investment (ROI). ITIL helps IT departments demonstrate their return on investment and measurable value to the business, and also cut IT costs. This helps establish a business case for new, or continuing, investment in IT.

- ITIL also helps in outsourcing. ITIL is widely practiced among many industry service providers and they can easily help your organisation's IT departments.

- Continuous improvement, stability and proactive problem prevention.

- Improved business image. Businesses will also learn what to commit, and what not to commit, to their external customers.

Important note

While ITIL has many benefits, it is not prescriptive. The important point is that the framework is independent of any IT vendors or their proprietary systems. As it is vendor neutral, it does not recommend or criticise any vendor's products or practices. This means ITIL will not tell you to use Microsoft® Windows® or buy Cisco® routers. Organisations are free to choose whatever IT equipment is best suited to their businesses. ITIL does not lay down any rigid guidelines or strict rules, but focuses on IT service management best practices that can be interpreted and used in various ways, or customised to your needs. You should understand what works in one company's IT environment may not work exactly the same in another. But even if your organisation implements only part of the ITIL framework, you can put your organisation on the road to becoming world class.

End result: Poor business and IT interaction

Figure 1: Before IT service management implementation

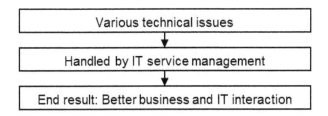

Figure 2: After IT service management implementation

How many departments are needed to implement IT service management or ITIL?

Professional IT service management, in any organisation, will involve several processes and functions over a period of time. Ideally, it is best to have separate departments to handle each process and function. However, it may not be possible, or affordable, for all organisations to build so many additional departments and personnel to handle all IT areas. If an organisation is big and has thousands of employees, then it is strongly recommended that it has separate departments with the workforce and budgets to handle their respective processes. If an organisation is small, then it will need to investigate whether it actually needs all the processes in the first place. A smaller organisation can choose to implement only a subset of all the processes, perhaps only the basic processes to begin with, and to have a diluted version of the others until it is necessary or affordable to implement them fully. Alternatively, it could have a single department with several managers who can become individual owners of each of the processes.

For example, IT services in RockSolid Corp (*see aforementioned example*) will consist of separate departments handling each of the processes. As a rule of thumb, small organisations can implement a workable ITIL set-up within three to nine months. Bigger organisations may take more than a year to implement essential ITIL. Fundamentally it depends on your internal speed, your willingness, and other political considerations you may need to overcome to truly implement such a framework.

How did ITIL start and evolve?

History of ITIL

During the late 1980s, the Central Computer and Telecommunications Agency (CCTA) started to work on a set of processes called the Information Technology Infrastructure Library (ITIL). Soon, many private and public companies adopted the framework and added their own best practices, and thus the ITIL framework became a set of industry best practices and a de facto standard in delivering IT services for all types of organisations.

In 2000, Microsoft® started using ITIL as the basis of the Microsoft® Operations Framework® (MOF) to support the launch of their Datacentre product.

In 2001, ITIL Version 2 was released with the Service Support and Service Delivery books.

In 2007, ITIL Version 3 was released (replacing Version 2) but it still included all the core principles and fundamentals of Version 2. Version 3 was organised around the concept of the service lifecycle, and included several new benefits to help businesses become world class.

By 2010, Version 2 and its certifications were fully withdrawn and Version 3 underwent various enhancements to meet industry requirements. It is now called ITIL 2011. However, ITIL officials have clarified that the ITIL 2011 edition is not a completely new version. In fact, it is only an update, but substantial content has been added to make ITIL easier to teach.

What were the main processes of ITIL Version 2?

ITIL Version 2 consisted of the following processes, each of which had many sub-processes:

- Service support
- Service delivery
- Planning to implement service management
- Applications management
- ICT infrastructure management
- The business perspective
- Security management.

Although Version 2 and its exams have been officially discontinued, this does not mean its concepts are outdated or useless.

What was ITIL Version 3?

Version 3 was an enhanced and improved version of Version 2 best practices. The structure and content of Version 3 was based on extensive public consultations and contributions from industry leaders, customers, users, vendors, service providers and other best practice organisations, to determine what improvements would make it suitable to modern, complex business requirements. However, this does not mean the concepts of ITIL Version 3 are outdated or useless because Version 3 was built on top of Version 2.

Version 3 had the following processes, each of which had many sub-processes and functions:

- Service strategy

- Service design
- Service transition
- Service operation
- Continual service improvement.

What is ITIL 2011?

ITIL 2011 is a substantial update to Version 3. This update was released to resolve certain inconsistencies in the documentation, fix some errors and address suggestions that were submitted by the training community. This book will essentially cover the processes of ITIL 2011 in more detail.

In summary, ITIL Version 2 has been phased out. The term ITIL 2007 is used for the first edition of ITIL Version 3. The latest edition is now referred to as ITIL 2011, or simply ITIL.

Table 1 briefly outlines the major difference between the various versions of ITIL

Table 1: Major differences between the various versions of ITIL

Version	Focus
2	Process based and operationally focused.
3	Value-based and business-focused service practice. Focuses on the alignment of IT and the business. Guides IT service management and organisations from just providing a great service, to becoming innovative and best in its class. A set of specialised organisational capabilities for providing value to customers in the form of services.
2011	ITIL 2011 is not a new version. It is only an update. This update was released to resolve certain inconsistencies in the documentation, fix some errors and address suggestions that were submitted by the training community for making ITIL easier to teach.

Will the books and training change with ITIL 2011?

Yes. New books have been released for ITIL 2011 editions. The official books can be purchased from IT Governance: *www.itgovernance.co.uk/ITIL-books.aspx*.

The new training courses and certification details can be obtained from the same website at: *www.itgovernance.co.uk/itsm_learning.aspx*.

Will the earlier ITIL concepts become invalid?

Not exactly, since the core principles won't change. However, you will not be able to take its exams anymore - ITIL 2011 has enhanced exams and certifications.

What are the latest ITIL exams or certifications today?

The following certifications are now available:

1. ITIL Foundation Certificate
2. ITIL Intermediate Certificate
3. ITIL Expert Certificate
4. ITIL Master Certificate.

Each of the above certifications are briefly explained below.

ITIL Foundation Certificate: This certificate is the introductory qualification for IT service management. The syllabus covers the terminology, processes and concepts of ITIL to provide a good grounding in ITIL principles. The ITIL Foundation exam is a 60 minute exam with 40 multiple choice questions. To pass you must score 65% or more (26/40). It can be taken online, or through an examination centre, or as part of a training course. This certification provides two credits toward your ITIL Expert certification.

ITIL Intermediate Certificate: This certificate evaluates an individual's ability to assess and apply the concepts of ITIL. The qualifications are organised around two streams – lifecycle and capability. The lifecycle stream is organised around the five core ITIL publications in the ITIL Lifecycle Publication Suite. By completing a lifecycle stream course you gain three credits toward the ITIL Expert certification. The capability stream is built around four practitioner-based clusters. Upon completing the relevant capability stream course, you will receive four credits toward your ITIL Expert certification.

ITIL Expert Certificate: The ITIL Expert certificate is automatically awarded to those who have achieved a total of 22 credits. Gaining the ITIL Expert certification demonstrates an individual's superior knowledge of the ITIL service lifecycle in its entirety. The 22 credits have to include credits from the mandatory Foundation and Managing Across the Lifecycle units, the other 15 credits can come from a variety of other Intermediate units prior to studying for the Managing Across the Lifecycle exam.

ITIL Master Certificate: The ITIL Master qualification is aimed at service management practitioners and consultants who are highly experienced at applying, managing and improving IT service management. To be eligible for the Master certificate, you must already possess an Expert certificate and have worked in IT service management for at least five years in leadership, management or higher management advisory level. The Master certificate will require candidates to explain and justify how they selected and applied a range of principles, knowledge, methods and techniques from ITIL, and other supporting management techniques, to accomplish business goals in multiple practical assignments.

What is meant by service in ITIL?

A service is a means of delivering value to customers by facilitating outcomes that customers want to achieve. The term 'service' is also used as a synonym for core service, IT service or service package.

What is the ITIL 2011 library?

The ITIL library is made up of five core books which are collectively known as the ITIL Lifecycle Publication Suite. The five core books are listed below.

1. Service Strategy
2. Service Design
3. Service Transition

4. Service Operation
5. Continual Service Improvement.

Each of these core books has multiple first level sub-processes, as outlined in the table below. There are also second level processes for many of the first level processes.

Table 2: Summary of ITIL 2011 Processes

CORE BOOK	SUB-PROCESSES
Service Strategy	1. Strategy management for IT services 2. Service portfolio management 3. Demand management 4. Financial management for IT services 5. Business relationship management
Service Design	1. Design coordination 2. Service catalogue management 3. Service level management 4. Risk management 5. Capacity management 6. Availability management 7. IT service continuity management 8. Information security management 9. Compliance management 10. Architecture management 11. Supplier management
Service Transition	1. Change management 2. Change evaluation 3. Project management 4. Application development 5. Release and deployment management 6. Service validation and testing 7. Service asset and configuration management 8. Knowledge management

CORE BOOK	SUB-PROCESSES
Service Operation	1. Event management 2. Incident management 3. Request fulfillment 4. Access management 5. Problem management 6. IT operations control 7. Facilities management 8. Application management 9. Technical management
Continual Service Improvement	1. Service review 2. Process evaluation 3. Definition of CSI initiatives 4. Monitoring of CSI initiatives

The first level sub-processes of each of the core books will be explained in the next chapter.

CHAPTER 3: THE ITIL LIFECYCLE

What is Service Strategy?

The objective of service strategy is to provide a plan (or strategy) to serve customers. This will assess customer needs, and the marketplace, to determine which services the organisation will offer, and what capabilities need to be developed. Service strategy largely relies upon a market-driven approach, and looks at what businesses need and don't need. It develops strategies to satisfy business needs, focuses on providing services that create business value and selects the appropriate strategy to deliver those services. Its ultimate goal is to make the IT organisation think and act in a strategic manner. It aligns the business and IT, so that each brings out the best in the other, instead of always, and traditionally, being at loggerheads with each other.

The ITIL definition of service strategy is as follows

'Service strategy defines the perspective, position, plans and patterns that a service provider needs to execute to meet an organisation's business outcomes.'

What are the sub-processes of service strategy?

Service strategy has the following sub-processes.

Strategy management for IT services: This process will evaluate, amongst other things, the IT service provider's offerings, capabilities, competitors and current and potential market spaces, to develop a strategy to serve customers. Once a strategy has been defined, this process is also responsible for ensuring the implementation of the strategy.

Assume that the telecommunications company (ABC-Telecom) servicing RockSolid Corp has introduced various new services, such as ultra-speed Internet, wireless local area networking and high resolution video conferencing. The service strategy process of RockSolid Corp will explore these new services to see if they can be adopted within their organisation, how it will be of value to the business, which might be the right departments to opt for this service and what other competitors are offering, and then decide on implementing immediately, or delaying it for a future date.

Service portfolio management: This process ensures that the service provider has the right mix of services that can be offered to its employees (customers) to meet required business outcomes with acceptable costs and ensure a return on investment. A service portfolio can be created by the IT service provider, outlining the existing services being offered now, new services being offered in the future, and also mention retired services that are no longer available. For example, the ABC-Telecom company servicing RockSolid Corp can claim to provide 2G and 3G as its existing services, and can also claim to provide 4G shortly, to lure and retain customers.

Demand management: This process understands, anticipates and influences customer demand for services. It is strategic in nature. Demand management works closely with capacity management (explained in *Chapter 12*) to ensure that the service provider has sufficient capacity to meet the required demands. Demand management plays a key role, as it aligns supply with demand and tries to forecast the sale of products and services as closely as possible.

Financial management for IT services: This process manages the service provider's budgeting, accounting and charging requirements. This is where IT employees learn the financial implications of their decisions, and what it costs the business to run and maintain IT. Financial management is required to channel investments to services that have the most potential. For example, when a service provider introduces a new service, or upgrades an existing service, this process starts by evaluating its financial impact and other aspects, such as budgeting for that service, accounting for how money was spent and how to charge customers for use of services.

Business relationship management: This process is designed to maintain a positive relationship with customers. It identifies the needs and desires of existing and potential customers, ensures that appropriate services are developed to meet those needs and builds customer relationships through value proposition. Many business case studies have proved that it costs a lot more to bring in new customers than to keep existing ones. A service provider may have top quality products and services, but if they can't keep their customers loyal, then that organisation will slowly wither away. The business relationship management process looks at all these aspects of retaining customers and makes appropriate changes on a regular basis. For example, ABC-Telecom can have one or more business relationship managers dedicated to service and retain RockSolid Corp.

What departments or staff are required for service strategy?

Any process will require dedicated staff and departments to implement and manage on a day-to-day basis. You cannot buy a dozen copies of ITIL books and distribute them to IT staff, and hope ITIL will be automatically implemented. Business managers must spend money and effort to create, and sustain, the necessary departments required to implement ITIL.

ITIL recommends the following kinds of roles, or staff, for implementing and managing service strategy.

Business relationship manager: This manager is responsible for maintaining good relationships with customers, identifying customer needs and ensuring that service providers are able to meet these needs with an appropriate catalogue of services. The business relationship manager works closely with the service level manager.

Demand manager: This manager is responsible for understanding, predicting and influencing customer demand for various services. He or she is also responsible for reallocating resources and equipment for maximum utilisation. The demand manager works closely with capacity management to ensure that the service provider has sufficient capacity to meet the required demand.

IT steering group (ISG): This group provides direction and strategy for IT services, and can include senior management from business and IT. The group reviews the business and IT strategies, in order to make sure that they are aligned. It also sets priorities for IT projects, to distinguish between must have projects and nice to have projects.

Financial manager: This manager is responsible for managing an IT service provider's budgeting, accounting and charging requirements.

Service strategy manager: This manager supports the IT steering group in producing, and maintaining, the service provider's strategy. This role is also responsible for communicating and implementing the service strategy.

Service portfolio manager: This manager provides a strategy to serve customers, and develops the service provider's offerings and capabilities.

For service strategy to produce results, all the above managers, and their team members, must cooperate and collaborate effectively, and not work in silos.

What is Service Design?

The objective of service design is to develop and design new, or changed, IT services, as well as incorporating changes and improvements to existing services. With good service design it is possible to deliver quality and cost-effective services to meet customer demands, reduce total cost of ownership (TCO), improve IT governance, strengthen customer satisfaction and explore innovative services that can be used for service excellence. In the absence of a good service design, technical services will evolve haphazardly, without taking into account current and future business needs. Any IT service provider that desires to deliver quality to customers must have the capability to design great services that meet the customer's expectations, and also aim to constantly exceed those expectations.

What are the sub-processes of service design?

Service design has the following sub-processes.

Design coordination: This process will coordinate all service design activities, processes and resources. It ensures the consistent and effective design of new, or changed, IT services, technology, architectures, processes, information and metrics.

Service catalogue management: This process ensures that a service catalogue (like a restaurant menu) is produced and maintained, containing current information on all services being offered and those being prepared to be run operationally.

Service level management: This process involves negotiating service levels, finalising the contents and periodically reviewing three key documents.

- Service level agreements (SLAs) negotiated with the business owners (customers according to ITIL, as explained previously).

- Operating level agreements (OLAs) negotiated with internal IT support groups, such as desktop support, network support and electrical facilities.

- Underpinning contracts (UCs) negotiated with external third-party suppliers, such as hardware and software vendors.

Risk management: This process identifies, assesses and controls risks. This includes analysing the value of assets to the business, identifying threats to those assets and evaluating how vulnerable each asset is to those threats.

Capacity management: This process ensures that the capacity (load handling) of the IT infrastructure and the IT services are able to deliver the agreed service level targets in a cost effective and timely manner. It also considers all resources required to deliver the IT service, and plans for short, medium and long term business requirements. Capacity management includes three sub-processes – business capacity management, service capacity management and component capacity management.

Availability management: This process is to define, analyse, plan, measure and improve all aspects of the availability (or uptime) of IT services. It is primarily to ensure that the promised levels of availability in all IT services are adhered to, or exceeded. This process is also responsible for ensuring that all IT infrastructure, processes, tools and roles are appropriate for the agreed availability targets.

IT service continuity management: This process is to manage risks that could seriously impact IT services, and to ensure service continuity in the event of disasters. Another goal is to maintain the necessary IT service continuity plans and IT recovery plans that support the organisational business continuity plans. It is also designed to support business continuity management[1].

Information security management: This process ensures the confidentiality, integrity and availability of an organisation's information, data and IT services.

Compliance management: This process ensures that IT services, processes and systems comply with enterprise policies and legal requirements.

Architecture management: This process defines a blueprint for the future development of the technical infrastructure of the organisation, taking into account various aspects, such as new technologies, market directions and service strategy.

---

[1] For more information on this refer to the book *Disaster Recovery and Business Continuity*, by the author (*www.itgovernance.co.uk/shop/p-520.aspx*).

Supplier management: Supplier management is responsible for managing all external third-party suppliers that provide, or support, IT services. This process ensures all contracts and agreements with suppliers support the needs of the business, and that all suppliers meet their contractual commitments.

What departments or staff are required for service design?

ITIL recommends the following roles, or staff, for implementing and managing service design.

Applications analyst: This role will manage applications throughout their lifecycle. Every key application will usually have one analyst, or a team of analysts. They will be involved in designing, testing, operating and improving IT services.

Capacity manager: This manager is responsible for ensuring that services and infrastructure are able to deliver the agreed capacity and performance targets in a cost effective and timely manner. This role will also plan for short, medium and long term business requirements, and the manager, or team, must work closely with the demand manager.

Availability manager: This manager is responsible for defining, analysing, planning, measuring and improving all aspects of the availability (uptime) of IT services. This person is also responsible for ensuring that all IT infrastructure, processes, tools and roles are appropriate for the agreed service level targets for availability.

Compliance manager: This manager will ensure that standards and guidelines are followed. This role will also make sure that legal requirements are fulfilled.

Enterprise architect: This person is responsible for maintaining the enterprise architecture (EA), which is a description of the essential components of a business and their interrelationships. Large organisations may have additional roles, such as business architect, application architect, information architect or infrastructure architect.

Information security manager: This manager is responsible for ensuring the confidentiality, integrity and availability of an organisation's assets, information, data and IT services.

Risk manager: This manager is responsible for identifying, assessing and controlling risks. This includes analysing the value of assets to the business, identifying threats to those assets, and evaluating how vulnerable each asset is to those threats.

IT service continuity manager: This manager is responsible for managing risks that could seriously impact IT services. He or she ensures that the IT service provider can provide minimum agreed service levels in cases of disaster, by reducing the risk to an acceptable level, and planning for the recovery of IT services.

Service catalogue manager: This manager is responsible for maintaining the service catalogue (explained in *Chapter 11*), and ensuring that all information within the service catalogue is accurate and up to date.

Service design manager: This manager is responsible for producing quality, secure and resilient designs for new, or improved, services. This includes producing and maintaining all design documentation.

Service level manager: This manager is responsible for negotiating service level agreements and ensuring that these are met. He or she makes sure that all IT service management processes, operational level agreements and underpinning contracts are appropriate for the agreed service level targets. The service level manager also monitors and reports on service levels.

Service owner: This person is responsible for delivering a particular service within the agreed service levels. Typically, he or she acts as the counterpart of the service level manager when negotiating operational level agreements (OLAs). The service owner may have a team of technical specialists, or an internal support unit.

Technical analyst: This role provides technical expertise and support for the management of the IT infrastructure. There is typically one technical analyst, or team of analysts, for every key technology area. This role plays an important part in the technical aspects of designing, testing, operating and improving IT services. It is also responsible for developing the skills required to operate the IT infrastructure.

Supplier manager: This manager is responsible for ensuring that value for money is obtained from all suppliers. He or she makes sure that contracts with suppliers support the needs of the business, and that all suppliers meet their contractual commitments.

For service design to produce results, all the above managers, and their team members, must cooperate and collaborate effectively, and not work in silos.

What is Service Operation?

The objective of ITIL service operation is to ensure that IT services are delivered effectively. Service operation is responsible for the 'business as usual' activities needed to maintain an IT infrastructure in peak condition. This includes the day-to-day jobs, such as attending to user requests, resolving service failures, fixing problems and carrying out routine operational tasks. From a customer's viewpoint, service operation is where value is seen. Service operation is aimed at IT managers, IT consultants, service practitioners, outsourcers and IT service vendors.

What are the sub-processes of service operation?

Service operations have the following sub-processes.

Event management: This process monitors CIs (configuration items – explained in *Chapter 9*) and services, and filters and categorises events in order to decide on appropriate actions. In ITIL terms, an 'event' is any detectable or discernible occurrence that has significance for the management of the IT infrastructure or the delivery of an IT service. Event management is the process responsible for detecting, managing and determining the appropriate control actions for these events throughout their lifecycle.

Incident management: This process manages the lifecycle of all incidents (explained in *Chapter 5*). The primary objective of incident management is to return the IT service to users as quickly as possible. This process is responsible for restoring service as quickly as possible and minimising adverse impacts of service interruptions.

Request fulfilment: This process fulfils service requests, which in most cases are minor changes (e.g. requests to change a password or install a computer), or requests for some advice or information. Service requests are managed by the request fulfilment process, usually in conjunction with the service desk (explained in *Chapter 4*).

Access management: This process grants authorised users the rights to use a service, while preventing access to non-authorised users. For example, access to a server that has confidential finance information cannot be provided to all employees, and must be allowed only for senior managers. The access management processes essentially execute policies defined in information security management. Access management is sometimes also referred to as 'rights management' or 'identity management'.

Problem management: This process manages the lifecycle of all problems (explained in *Chapter 6*). The primary objectives of problem management are to prevent incidents from happening, and to minimise the impact of incidents that cannot be prevented. It prevents problems to IT services, eliminates recurring incidents, identifies the root cause of service interruptions and proposes permanent fixes to eliminate this cause. Proactive problem management analyses incident records, and uses data collected by other IT service management processes to identify trends or significant problems. This process also submits a request for change that will implement temporary or permanent fixes to various problems.

IT operations control: This process monitors and controls the IT services and their underlying infrastructure. The process IT operations control executes day-to-day routine tasks related to the operation of infrastructure components and applications. This includes job scheduling, back-up and restore activities, disk space management, print and output management and routine computer maintenance activities. These operational actions emphasise executing repeatable, standardised procedures.

Facilities management: This process manages the physical environment where the IT infrastructure is located. Facilities management includes all aspects of managing the physical environment, such as power and cooling, building access management and environmental monitoring.

Application management: This process is responsible for managing applications throughout their lifecycle. This supports and maintains various operational applications that are required for an organisation to do its business. It also helps in identifying the functionality and manageability requirements for software in the application portfolio, and then assists in the deployment, support and improvement of those applications.

Technical management: This process provides technical expertise and support for the management of the IT infrastructure. The objectives of this function are to plan, implement and maintain a stable, technical infrastructure to support the business processes of the enterprise. This includes training and deploying appropriate personnel to build and operate the technology required to deliver and support IT services.

What departments or staff are required for service operations?

ITIL recommends the following roles for implementing and managing service operations.

First level support: The responsibility of this team is to register and classify received incidents, and to undertake an immediate effort in order to restore a failed IT service as quickly as possible. If no quick solution can be achieved, the first level support will transfer the incident to expert technical support groups (second level support). First level support also processes service requests, and keeps users informed about their incident status at agreed intervals.

Second level support: This team will take over incidents that cannot be solved immediately by first level support. If necessary, they will request external support from software or hardware manufacturers. The aim is to restore a failed IT service as quickly as possible. If no solution can be found, the second level support passes on the incident to problem management.

Third level support: This support is typically located at hardware or software manufacturers (third-party suppliers). Its services are requested by second level support if required for solving an incident. The aim is to restore a failed IT service as quickly as possible.

Access manager: The access manager grants authorised users the right to use a service, while preventing access to non-authorised users. The access manager essentially executes policies defined in information security management.

Facilities manager: This manager is responsible for managing the physical environment where the IT infrastructure is located. This includes all aspects of managing the physical environment, such as power and cooling, building access management and environmental monitoring.

Incident manager: This manager is responsible for the effective implementation of the incident management process and its reporting. They represent the first stage of escalation for incidents, in case they are not resolved within the agreed service levels.

IT operations manager: This manager will be responsible for overall responsibility for a number of service operation activities. For instance, this role will ensure that all day-to-day operational activities are carried out in a timely and reliable way.

IT operator: Staff in this role will perform the day-to-day operational activities. Typical responsibilities will include activities such as server back-ups, scheduling jobs and installing equipment inside data centres.

Major incident team: This is a technical expert team used for the resolution of major incidents.

Problem manager: This manager is responsible for managing the lifecycle of all problems. Their primary objectives are to prevent incidents from happening, and to minimise the impact of incidents that cannot be prevented. For this purpose, they will maintain information about known errors and workarounds.

Service request fulfilment group: This group specialises in fulfilling certain types of service requests. Typically, first level support will process simpler requests, while others are forwarded to such specialised fulfilment groups.

What is Service Transition?

The objective of service transition is to build and deploy IT services. Service transition also makes sure that changes to services and processes are carried out in a coordinated way. Service transition is responsible for managing the complexity of a large number of changes and associated deployments for new or modified services. From a practical perspective, service transition involves packaging, building, testing and deploying a release (e.g. a software upgrade) into production, and a rollback if necessary.

What are the sub-processes of service transition?

Service transition has the following sub-processes.

Change management: This process controls the lifecycle of all changes. Change management is responsible for the monitoring and control of changes to the infrastructure. It oversees authorising, prioritising, planning, scheduling, testing and implementing new IT services or major changes to existing services.

Change evaluation: This process evaluates major changes, such as the introduction of a new service or a major change to an existing service, before they are allowed to be implemented on the infrastructure. The purpose of this process is to determine whether the actual performance of a new or changed service compares favourably to predicted performance, and whether it operates acceptably by providing value to the customer.

Project management: This process is responsible for planning and coordinating the resources to deploy any new or major changes and releases within the predicted cost, time and quality estimates.

Application development: This process is to make available various applications and systems that provide the required functionality for IT services. It also includes the development and maintenance of custom applications, and customisation of products from software vendors.

Release and deployment management: These processes are for planning, scheduling and controlling the movement of releases to test and live environments.

- Release management is responsible for planning, scheduling and controlling the implementation of new or changed services in the form of a release package. It covers releases for both testing and production environments. The primary goal of release management is to ensure that the integrity of the live environment is protected, and that the correct components are released.

- Deployment management is responsible for the movement of new or changed hardware, software, documentation or other configuration items, into the live production environment.

Service validation and testing: This process ensures that the deployed releases and the resulting services meet customer expectations, and verifies if the IT operations are able to support the new service. It ensures that the outputs of service design and the release package will deliver a new or changed service that adds value to the customer. It also ensures that it is fit for purpose and fit for use. This process confirms these assurances through thorough validation and testing procedures.

Service asset and configuration management: This process maintains information about configuration items (CIs) required to deliver an IT service and their interrelationships. It provides a logical model of the IT infrastructure, consisting of configuration items, their attributes and their relationships.

Knowledge management: This process gathers, analyses, stores and shares knowledge and information within an organisation. This process ensures that the right information is provided to the appropriate individuals in a timely manner, enabling them to make informed decisions about the future expansion, contraction or revision of IT services. The primary purpose of knowledge management is to improve efficiency by reducing the need to rediscover knowledge.

What departments or staff are required for service transition?

ITIL recommends the following kinds of roles for implementing and managing service transition.

Application developer: This person is responsible for making applications and systems that provide the required functionality for IT services. This also includes the development and maintenance of custom applications, as well as the customisation of products from software vendors.

Change advisory board (CAB): This team, or board, is for advising the change manager in the assessing, prioritising and scheduling of changes on the infrastructure. This board is usually made up of representatives from all areas within the IT organisation, the business and third parties, such as suppliers.

Change manager: This manager controls the lifecycle of all changes. Their primary objective is to enable beneficial changes to be made, with minimum disruption to IT services. For important changes, the change manager will refer the authorisation of changes to the change advisory board (CAB).

Configuration manager: This manager is responsible for maintaining information about configuration items required to deliver IT services. They will also maintain a logical model, containing the components of the IT infrastructure (CIs) and their associations.

Emergency change advisory board (ECAB): This is a subset of the change advisory board which makes decisions about high-impact emergency changes. The membership for this team may be decided at the time a meeting is called, and depends on the nature of the emergency change.

Knowledge manager: This manager ensures that the IT organisation is able to gather, analyse, store and share knowledge and information. Their primary goal is to improve efficiency by reducing the need to rediscover knowledge.

Project manager: This role is responsible for planning and coordinating the resources to deploy a major release within the predicted cost, time and quality estimates.

Release manager: This person is responsible for planning and controlling the movement of releases to test and live environments. Their primary objective is to ensure that the integrity of the live environment is protected, and that the correct and trouble-free components are released.

Test manager: This manager ensures that deployed releases and the resulting services meet customer expectations, and verifies that IT operations are able to support the new service.

What is Continual Service Improvement?

Any infrastructure or service cannot be stagnant for months and years at a certain level. It will always need tweaks, improvements and upgrades, without which the business cannot be trouble free, modern or competitive. This process is taken care of by continual service improvement (CSI). CSI will provide guidance in creating and maintaining value for customers through better design and more efficient operation of services. This CSI process uses methods from quality management in order to learn from past successes and failures. It is also important to note that the word 'continual' is used, instead of continuous. Continual means a process runs for a duration of time at a certain standard and then gets interrupted for a change or improvement. In continual improvement, you will notice some improvements in stages. For example, a turnaround time of three hours may be maintained by the IT department for support issues, for some months, and then they may decide to improve it to two hours turnaround time because of other technical improvements and staff increases. On the other hand, continuous means uninterrupted or unceasing in a grammatical sense. A continuous service improvement will theoretically mean there is some improvement every day and every minute which is practically impossible, and usually the dream of idealistic workaholics.

What are the sub-processes of continual service improvement?

Continual service improvement has the following sub-processes.

Service review: This process reviews business and infrastructure services on a regular basis. The aim of this process is to improve service quality and identify more economical ways of providing services, wherever possible or necessary.

Process evaluation: This involves evaluating various processes on a regular basis. This includes identifying areas where the targeted process metrics are not reached, and holding regular benchmarking, audits, maturity assessments and reviews.

Definition of CSI initiatives: This process will define specific initiatives aimed at improving services and processes, based on service reviews and process evaluations. The resulting initiatives can be internal or external by involving a supplier or vendor.

Monitoring of CSI initiatives: This process verifies if the improvement initiatives are proceeding according to plan, and introduces corrective measures wherever necessary.

What departments or staff are required for continual service improvement?

ITIL recommends the following kinds of roles for implementing and managing CSI.

CSI manager: This manager is responsible for managing improvements to the IT service management processes and IT services. They will continually measure the performance of the service provider, and design improvements to processes, services and infrastructure, to improve efficiency, effectiveness and cost effectiveness.

Process architect: This person is responsible for maintaining the process architecture (part of the enterprise architecture), coordinating all changes to processes and making sure that all processes cooperate in a seamless way. This role may also support various parties involved in managing and improving processes, in particular the process owners.

Process owner: This role is responsible for ensuring that a process is fit for purpose. Their responsibilities will include sponsorship, design and continual improvement of the process and its metrics. In larger organisations there may be separate process owner and process manager roles, where the process manager has responsibility for the operational management of a process.

CHAPTER 4: SERVICE DESK FUNCTION

'Business is not just doing deals; business is having great products, doing great engineering and providing tremendous service to customers. Finally, business is a cobweb of human relationships.'

Ross Perot

What is a service desk?

A service desk is usually a single point of contact for your business managers and end-users to reach the IT department, for resolving all their IT issues or technical troubles. This is where all questions, issues and requests are logged, recorded and followed through until closure. A service desk is a functional unit consisting of a number of dedicated staff responsible for dealing with service events, usually made via telephone, e-mail or the Web. The type of service desk you need depends on the requirements of your end-user base. A business can have several service desks for different areas: computers, telecommunications, software, information only, etc. Service desks are also sometimes known by other names, e.g. help desks, call centres and technical assistance.

The ITIL definition of a service desk is:

'The single point of contact between the service provider and the users. A typical service desk manages incidents and service requests, and also handles communication with the users.'

Why do you need a service desk?

The answer to this question is twofold. First, you need to understand what will happen to your organisation if you don't have a service desk. Second, you need to understand how your organisation will benefit from having a service desk.

Let us take the first scenario. Thousands of employees can tell countless horror stories regarding various internal support issues within their own organisations. Each of these stories can directly or indirectly impact your business. If your internal employees are unable to work due to computer, network or IT troubles, then your organisation cannot conduct its business or meet your external customer demands. The hassles your end-users and your business will suffer from without a service desk are illustrated in this example:

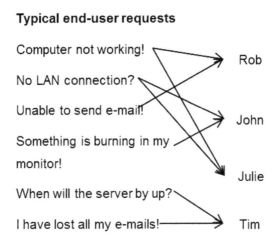

Typical end-user requests

Computer not working!

No LAN connection?

Unable to send e-mail!

Something is burning in my monitor!

When will the server by up?

I have lost all my e-mails!

Rob

John

Julie

Tim

Figure 3: Before service desk implementation

Now let us take the second scenario. Having a professional service desk adds value to your end-users and business managers. It helps in resolving incidents quickly, monitoring progress and logging of all user requests, tracking until resolution.

Typical end-user requests

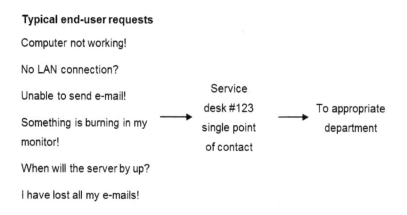

Computer not working!

No LAN connection?

Unable to send e-mail!

Something is burning in my monitor!

When will the server by up?

I have lost all my e-mails!

Service desk #123 single point of contact

To appropriate department

Figure 4: After service desk implementation

What are the responsibilities of a service desk?

As mentioned earlier, the service desk is a single point of contact for end-users who need help on IT issues, so its responsibilities are enormous, as everything they do (or don't do) can affect the business. Having a professional service desk will generate business benefits, such as improved end-user satisfaction, quick turnaround on requests, improved business image, improved employee productivity and faster solutions to IT-related issues. For the end-user, the advantage is that they don't have to ring or contact several people to solve their issues, and for IT personnel it means that they only have to concentrate on technical areas they are skilled in. Without this single point of contact, any organisation would face major losses in time and money spent on looking for ways to fix issues and get help.

The value of a service desk cannot, and should not, be underestimated. A service desk has the following main responsibilities:

- Being the first point of contact for end-users and business owners. They handle all incoming calls and route them to second or third level support if necessary.

- Receiving and logging all support requests.

- Prioritising calls based on severity, or seriousness, of the fault.

- Escalating and routing support requests to appropriate departments.

- Keeping end-users informed about their call status and progress.

- Following up until call closure. The service desk is the owner until closure.

- Necessary reporting.

What are the different types of service desk?

Depending on company size and need, a typical service desk can be designed in various flavours, such as those examples that follow.

- **Basic help desk**: A call centre manned by secretarial and non-technical staff that receive calls and pass them to appropriate technical divisions. These personnel can simply note down an error on an end-user's computer and then send a qualified person to fix it.

- **Medium help desk**: A semi-skilled help desk that can provide small to medium solutions over the phone, and other support access methods. Such personnel can instruct the end-user to try this, or that, to see how a trouble or issue can be fixed.

- **Advanced help desk**: A fully-skilled or expert help desk that can provide complete customer and user assistance. In many organisations they can even remotely log on to an end-user's computer and fix various issues, configure settings and interact with users to resolve troubles.

- **Request fulfilment centre**: A service desk, or a portion of it, can also act as a service request fulfilment centre. A service request is anything other than an incident. As explained earlier, the request fulfilment process is defined as managing non-incident related service requests. In practical terms, a service request is a formal request from a user for something, such as some information or advice, or to reset a password, or to install a computer for a new user.

Each of the above can be further organised in various ways, including:

- Centralised service desk

- Distributed or local service desk

- Virtual service desk

- Mixed service desk.

A *centralised* service desk is suitable for some organisations and types of support where it makes sense to keep it centralised. This can result in lower costs, and avoids duplication of facilities, skills and procedures. A *distributed* or *local* service desk is suitable for organisations which have branches in various locations, requirements for immediate local support or, for political reasons. A *virtual* service desk can be located anywhere in the world, with a third-party vendor providing support to your organisation from their office elsewhere. This is suitable for various types of businesses, such as software application support and Internet-based support. Such desks can be established using advanced telecommunication and network technologies. It is also possible to establish a *mixed* service desk that can combine two or more of the above desks, for maximum flexibility. A small, essential on-site service desk can coordinate with a large service desk at the central site. However, there are no single, universal service desk models that will suit every organisation. Businesses will have to study, and implement, the best possible service desk to run their businesses smoothly, and increase revenues.

What options should be provided to contact your service desk?

End-users must be able to get their IT troubles and issues fixed quickly, as no work can be done these days without IT. This can be done only if each and every end-user knows how to contact the service desk quickly to get their issues resolved. Imagine an end-user in your organisation having a computer breakdown and not knowing who to call for support. Suppose you call the technical department and the call gets routed from desk to desk without anybody taking responsibility for understanding your needs. Just imagine your hassles. To avoid this, you should ensure that every employee in your organisation know how to reach the service desk. Service desks must have more than one method for users to reach them, as illustrated here:

- Business and end-users can call a single number, e.g. #123, to contact the service desk.

- Business and end-users can send an e-mail, e.g. to *servicedesk@rocksolid.com*.

- Business and end-users can visit the technical department and contact someone directly.

- Business and end-users can log support requests via a support website, e.g. *http://support.intranet.com*.

- Business and end-users can fax support requests to a support fax number, e.g. 888 8888, or a pager, e.g. 7777.

- Business and end-users can call an individual, e.g. Paul on 0800 135 4678, or Rick on 0800 124 5679, for all support-related issues between 9 am and 5 pm, Monday to Friday. After-hours support can be found by calling Kim on 0800 246 7292.

What tools and equipment do service desk personnel need?

Apart from technical training and customer-handling techniques, personnel in a professional service desk department need two main types of equipment and tools.

They will need communication equipment to help end-users contact the service desk. For example:

- Advanced telephone systems with features, such as call-hunting, auto-answer, auto-routing, message-recording and music on hold.

- Auto-answering machines.

- Fax, e-mail, and SMS services.

- A private toll-free number.

- A unique e-mail ID for end-users to send e-mail, if possible, for requesting support.

Next, the service desk will require appropriate tools, software and equipment to assist end-users and solve IT issues:

- Call-logging and help desk tools and software.

- Knowledge-base software which can be continuously updated by support staff and viewed by service desk and other personnel. This can be especially helpful in service desk personnel being able to solve many routine and simple issues over the phone.

- Manuals, flowcharts, troubleshooting tips, etc.

- Network management tools.

- Video systems.

- Remote management tools.

The cost of implementing such tools and facilities can range from a few thousand pounds to several hundred thousand, depending on the size of the organisation. Huge organisations cannot have small, nursery tools to provide service desk support to their thousands of employees. They will need high-end systems that can handle and track thousands of support calls, so they invest in enterprise and heavy-duty systems and associated software. The type of tool you need is fully dependent on what you want to get out of it. For small organisations, the tool can even be a simple Excel spreadsheet. For larger organisations, you will probably be looking at heavy-duty service desk tools. However, irrespective of the organisation's size, always ensure that you keep it simple. Just because you have selected a feature-rich, complex tool, does not mean you have implemented the best service desk. Organisations must first design their internal processes, before they start searching for a tool. If the processes are simple, buy a simple tool and use it to the maximum possible. If a simple tool is not available, it is possible to build a customised tool with the help of software programmers. Always select a tool that is simple and neat. Some tools are extremely complicated and have hundreds of features and reporting facilities that will probably never be used in the lifetime of the product.

Most companies provide service desk software. You can download free evaluation copies of their software to install and explore the product. Once you have decided on a tool, be fully informed and knowledgeable about the following:

- Complete product and add-on prices
- Hidden costs – read the small print carefully
- Licensing costs
- Maintenance costs
- Warranty
- Support and training requirements for the tool itself
- Upgrades and patches for the tools
- Implementation costs
- How to extract the reports you need
- Performance tuning and training for the tools.

A typical, simple help desk software screen that many service desks use is shown in Figure 5. The example shown has details of an unresolved, but assigned, support call.

RockSolid Corp Service Desk System			
Call #	IN-32	**User Call Time**	9:45
User	Richard	**SLA Commitment**	3 hours
Department	Sales	**Assigned to**	Paul at 10
Phone #	490	**Completed Time**	
Floor	3rd Floor	**Status**	Open
Building	Main	**Priority**	Medium
Type	Printer	**Charges**	Nil
Asset #		**Other Info**	
Call Details		**Resolution Details**	
Printer not working			

Figure 5: A typical, simple, help desk software screenshot

Are there any ITIL-compliant software or hardware?

No, ITIL does not certify any vendor's software or hardware as ITIL compliant. It only makes recommendations for IT service best practices. Although vendors may make marketing claims that their products are ITIL compliant, officially, the owners of ITIL will not give any certificate of compliance to any hardware or software product.

What job roles are needed in a service desk department?
Just like any department, a service desk department needs managers and operational staff. A typical service desk department can have the following personnel. Of course, clearly drafted and agreed job descriptions, responsibilities and empowerment should be provided to run any department successfully.

1. **Service desk manager:** Responsible for overall desk activities, acts as an escalation point, reports to senior management on issues that could impact the business, attends business meetings, changes review meetings, becomes the department's leader, arranges staff trainings and takes the heat for the team.

2. **Service desk supervisor:** Small organisations may not have a manager. Instead, they may have just a supervisor with some, or all, of the responsibilities outlined above. Alternatively, a service desk manager may find it necessary to have a few supervisors report to him or her, to take care of shift operations or balance the workload. The manager can concentrate on pure business matters, while the supervisors can do the job of looking after the service analysts, and follow the instructions of the manager.

3. **Service desk analysts:** These are the actual lower-rung staff that answer the phones, reply to e-mails from end-users and route calls to appropriate specialist departments. They are the ones who will assign a call number to end-users, take ownership and follow through until closure, and also the people who get shouted at by end-users.

Some tips and advice for a responsive service desk

Your organisation cannot be called 'professional' unless you implement industry-standard best practices. As the name suggests, best practices help you become the best in your area. Some useful best practices and tips to establish a professional service desk are as follows:

- Business managers must ensure that they regularly check whether their service desk is in proper working order. For example, a business owner, or a CEO, can simply impersonate an end-user or a customer and try to call their own company's service desk, to find out the service quality (or horror experiences) of their own company.

- Essential training must be provided to service desk personnel to do their job well. This training is a combination of hard and soft skills. Hard skills will be the standard technical training they need. Soft skills will be elements, such as stress management, customer handling techniques, effective written and verbal communication, documentation skills and understanding business criticality. The more knowledge they have, the better the support and service will be.

- Adequate staff ratio. This means the number of service desk staff should be a proper percentage of the number of end-users they can support. You cannot have just two service desk staff to answer support calls from a network having a thousand computer users. A bad staff ratio will only worsen your business, as the staff will resign frequently, or give bad service. You should also consider things, such as providing more staff during peak times, for example on Monday mornings, or during busy seasons when user calls will peak.

- Ensure that the service desk is situated in a low noise environment, with proper lighting and resting facilities. A good library of useful books and soft music will also help.

- Service desk personnel must be taught to be professional and courteous in their service, even if end-users are rude, which can happen quite frequently.

- Periodically conduct a formal, or informal, survey among service staff to find out their work-related issues, and take measures to implement and solve whatever is possible.

- Simply establishing a service desk and overloading it with every best practice available is not called a professional service desk. The workload must be reasonable and appropriate. For this, a service desk department must have a proper, mutually agreed service level agreement with the business. Here the service objectives, goals and deliverables must be clearly defined. Next, you should ensure the service levels are practical, agreed and regularly reviewed. Business managers must allocate the necessary budgets to improve services, new tools, equipment and good recommendations. Involve service desk personnel in business meetings to mutually understand each other's needs, expectations, requirements and limitations.

- Metrics should be established so that the performance of the service desk can be evaluated at regular intervals. This is important to assess the health, maturity, efficiency and effectiveness of your service desk. The service desk manager or supervisor should be responsible for this; it will prove to your business, and your end-users, that you have a responsible and professional service desk. The metrics you choose must be meaningful, and help you to improve services. Quantitative measurements are no proof of superior quality service. There is no use boasting that your service desk will pick up every phone call within three rings, and then give the number of calls that were picked within and outside three rings as a metric. You could pick up within three rings but you could also be giving bad solutions or improper advice. So service should be quality based and not numerically fancy.

- Other metrics, such as average time to resolve an incident, time to escalate an incident, service desk costs, percentage of end-users making use of the service desk, number of calls per day and per hour, can also be measured and documented.

- Service desk jobs are very stressful and cause employees to burn out very quickly. This is because it involves a constant stream of end-users pouring their woes and grievances out on the service desk. Some end-users can also be very rude, so ensure that the working hours are limited. Best results can be achieved if desk staff work no more than four to five hours a day in such jobs.

Important Note

It is not just the service desk personnel that need to be trained how to operate a service desk. Even end-users must be taught the etiquette of how to use their service desk. No end-user must take the service desk for granted, monopolise the services, or be rude to staff. End-users must be trained to recognise what constitutes a business emergency and must be taught to understand that not every IT issue constitutes a top priority call to demand immediate attention, or harass the service desk staff.

CHAPTER 5: INCIDENT MANAGEMENT

'There is more to life than simply increasing its speed.'

Mahatma Gandhi

What is an incident?

An incident is any event that causes, or may cause, an interruption to the quality of an agreed IT service. For example, a power supply failure in a user's computer, a user logon ID locking up, a user not being able to access a web server or an e-mail system, are all classified as incidents.

The ITIL definition of an incident is:

'An unplanned interruption to an IT service or a reduction in the quality of an IT service. Failure of a configuration item that has not yet impacted service is also an incident. For example, failure of one disk from a mirror set.'

Isn't an incident the same as a problem?

No. In ITIL language, the word 'problem' has a different meaning, and hence it should not be used casually. A problem is a pattern of incidents, or an incident for which there is no immediate solution. This will be covered in the next chapter, which tries to identify the root causes of incidents and recommend necessary changes.

What is incident management?

Incident management is part of the service operation phase of the ITSM core lifecycle. The goal of incident management is to restore normal service operation as quickly as possible, and minimise any adverse impact on business operations. When a user experiences any IT troubles, the incident management process, or team, will ensure that the user's service is restored as soon as possible, using a temporary workaround if necessary. This is to get the end-user, and the business, back to normal as soon as possible. It is symptom driven, and the only concern is speed of response and the continuation of the business.

The ITIL definition of incident management is:

'The process responsible for managing the lifecycle of all incidents. Incident management ensures that normal service operation is restored as quickly as possible and the business impact is minimised.'

All incidents must be recorded. An incident record is:

A record containing the details of an incident. Each incident record documents the lifecycle of a single incident.

What are the responsibilities of incident management?

Some of the main responsibilities of incident management are as follows:

• Attend to the incident as soon as possible.

• Alert specialist support groups or vendors if they cannot solve the incident.

• Keep the end-user and service desk informed about the status of the call.

• Classify incidents according to type and priority, and match against a known error, or previously attended incident. A known error is some incident for which there is a solution.

- Inform the problem management department if new incidents are discovered, or the incident is not in the known errors list.

- Try to resolve the incident using readily available solutions, or provide a workaround until the incident can be sorted out properly.

- Close the incident.

Why is incident management necessary?

Any large IT infrastructure will have several computers, network and related troubles, during the course of its operations. The troubles could be minor, medium or major. End-users will require some immediate technical assistance to resolve the issue. This is where incident management will help. An incident management team is a sort of rapid action team, whose main responsibility is to fix troubles immediately, using known solutions or workarounds. The root, or real cause, of why such computer troubles are occurring in the IT infrastructure, is handled by a specialist problem management team (covered in *Chapter 6*).

Example: Incident management attending an issue

Finance Manager: 'Hello, Service Desk. All our finance servers are not responding. Please send someone immediately.'

Incident Management: Hello, I'm from the Incident Management team. What seems to be the issue?'

Finance Manager: 'All our finance servers are not responding.'

Incident Management: 'Okay. Looks like the servers have locked-up. Simple. I will just reset them and you will be able to work again.'

Finance Manager: 'You'd better fix this trouble soon. We've been having this issue very often over the last few weeks. We are losing important data.'

Incident Management: 'Very often? Then let me inform our specialist team to investigate.'

What is incident priority?

A general dictionary defines priority as *'precedence, especially established by order of importance or urgency'*. As with any other types of service, incidents have priorities. Obviously, all incidents cannot be given the same importance or urgency. Resolution of certain incidents can wait, while others cannot. Incidents are classified according to pre-determined priorities. The service desk determines the priorities of incidents as it receives them. Different organisations use different methods of priorities:

- High, low, medium

- Immediate, urgent, moderate, ordinary

- Severity 1, 2, 3, 4 (1 being the most urgent)

- Critical, medium, routine.

Realistic categories and turnaround times have to be prepared in consultation with the business, customers and end-users. Incident management should not commit that they will attend every incident within ten minutes, just to impress everyone. It is neither sustainable nor advisable. It is always recommended to categorise incidents based on *'business impact'*, which means that any incident that may affect business will get higher priority. Prioritisation is necessary for allocating resources and staff properly. Otherwise, staff could be busy attending a routine incident, whilst an urgent incident may be waiting unresolved.

What is a business impact?

A business impact is anything that affects, or has the potential to disrupt, the business, as shown in Table 3. The examples you select in the table must be specific to your business. For example, Company 1 may classify their e-mail system not working as 'high priority', and their fax machine not working as 'low priority'. However, Company 2 may classify their fax machine not working as 'high priority', and their e-mail system not working as 'low priority'.

Table 3: Business impact classifications

Priority	Impact	Examples
High	• Disruption to business • Critical • Emergencies • Stops end-users or customers from working • Needs immediate and continuous action to resolve or give a workaround	Enter your organisation-defined examples
Medium	• General end-user and customer support • Day-to-day tech support • Routine calls	Enter your organisation-defined examples
Low	• Non-technical support • Low priority tasks	Enter your organisation-defined examples

What is an incident category?

In addition to business priorities for incidents, they also have to be categorised according to equipment, end-users, etc. Typical examples of categorisation include:

- Desktop computer incidents
- Server computer incidents
- Telecommunication incidents
- Software incidents
- Security violation incidents
- Virus incidents
- Password issues (can be routed to request fulfilment)
- New requests (can be routed to request fulfilment).

Each of these can have sub-incidents and priorities, as mentioned earlier.

Typical examples of incidents

Some typical examples are:

- Users unable to access a server
- A machine not booting-up
- A virus attack on a machine
- A file corruption
- A hardware fault on some equipment
- General user issues and queries.

How can IT services reduce the number of incidents?

As an organisation grows in terms of staff and IT equipment, the service desk and incident management team will be inundated with support calls. However, many of the calls will be of a routine and simple nature that can be easily solved by end-users themselves, with a little bit of training and some self-service options. IT services can drastically reduce the number of common and routine incidents by creating a self-service model:

- User education and training.

- Providing a 'How do I?' or FAQ (Frequently Asked Questions) list to end-users.

- Providing solutions to common incidents via the company intranet, or e-mail, or phone.

- Providing tips through e-mail, newsletters, etc.

- Identifying cooperative staff within various departments to assist their own department members for certain types of incident. For example, a sales secretary can learn how to assist in changing the user's password for all the sales department staff, or configure a mail profile or a printer, when required.

- Design and secure the network and systems such that ordinary end-users cannot fiddle around or experiment with their systems.

- Organisations can also explore rotating staff between a service desk and incident management. For example, a techie who has worked for some time in the incident team can provide a superior, service desk support. This is because he or she can immediately recognise common IT troubles and give solutions directly over the phone, based on his or her past on-site experience, often without having to visit the end-user's workplace.

What is classification matching?

As support calls arrive, they must be matched with the known error database (explained in *Chapter 6*), to see if any incidents with the same, or similar symptoms, already exist. It is like looking into a dictionary with a specific word in hand. If an incident cannot be matched, then it is classified as a new incident, and must be investigated until a resolution or a workaround is found.

What is incident routing?

Service desk and incident personnel may not have all the skills, tools or knowledge to solve every type of service request related to their businesses. Other specialist departments are required to assist the service desk in finally resolving the end-user's issues. These specialist departments can also be called second-level, or third-level, support groups. The service desk is the first level of support and owner of all incidents for an end-user. Proper documented and agreed arrangements have to be established between the various levels, to ensure that the business and end-users do not have inordinate delays or gaps in support. Incident routing must be a documented and agreed arrangement.

What is incident escalation?

Incident routing is a horizontal flow that happens because the service desk is usually not in a position to resolve all requests. Incident escalation, on the other hand, is a vertical flow that has management and senior management involvement. Escalations are sometimes necessary because of major incidents, or angry end-users that may directly contact a senior person and report their issues. For example, a user may contact the service desk for a simple incident, and because of the delay in resolution, or some other reason, may complain to a senior manager, bypassing the regular routes. Alternatively, the service desk or second/third level staff may also escalate some incident or issue to a senior manager, due to the authority required in taking decisions.

What is an incident lifecycle?

An incident lifecycle is the progress of an incident from start to closure. The entire cycle consists of:

- Occurrence of the incident (e.g. e-mail server not switching on).

- Detection of the incident (e.g. an end-user reporting it to the service desk, who in turn classify the incident as high priority and call the incident management team).

- Diagnosis of the cause of failure (e.g. failed power supply).

- Repair of the configuration item (CI) (e.g. repair of the mail server by replacing the power supply). A CI is any component of an IT infrastructure, e.g. the e-mail server itself is a CI. CIs are covered later in *Chapter 9*.

- Restoration of the service.

- Closure of the incident, with necessary documentation and reporting.

A simple incident management report is as follows:

Table 4: A simple incident management report

Call number	IN-32
Service desk	Call received by Laura of Service Desk at 9:45 am
Assigned to	Paul of Incident Team
End-user	Mr Richards, 3rd Floor, Sales Dept, #490
Summary	Printer not working
Call assigned time	10 am, Monday 16 July
Call attended time	11 am, Monday 16 July
Committed SLA	3 hours. Response within three hours of end-user call time
Call effort	Took ten minutes to resolve trouble
Resolution details	Printer cable was disconnected. Connected it properly. Printer OK.
Status	Call closed

After resolving, Paul can inform the service desk to close the call.

What are the sub-processes of incident management?

Incident management has the following sub-processes.

Incident management support: This process will provide, and maintain, the tools, processes, skills and rules required for an effective and efficient handling of incidents.

Incident logging and categorisation: This process records and prioritises the incident with appropriate diligence, in order to facilitate a swift and effective resolution.

Immediate incident resolution by first level support: This process will solve an incident within the agreed time schedule. The aim is the fast recovery of the IT service, where necessary with the aid of a workaround. If that first level support is unable to resolve the incident itself, or when target times for first level resolution are exceeded, the incident is transferred to a suitable group within second level support.

Incident resolution by second level support: This process will solve an incident within the agreed time schedule. The aim is the fast recovery of the service, even if they have to use a workaround. If required, specialist support groups or third-party suppliers (third level support) are involved. If the correction of the root cause is not possible, a problem record is created and the error-correction transferred to problem management.

Handling of major incidents: The objective of this process is to resolve a major incident. Major incidents cause serious interruptions of business activities, and must be resolved with greater urgency. The aim is the fast recovery of the service, even if they have to use a workaround. If required, specialist support groups or third-party suppliers are involved. If the correction of the root cause is not possible, a problem record is created and the error-correction transferred to problem management.

Incident monitoring and escalation: This process will continuously monitor the processing status of outstanding incidents, so that countermeasures may be introduced as soon as possible if service levels are likely to be breached.

Incident closure and evaluation: This process will submit the incident record to a final quality control before it is closed. The aim is to make sure that the incident is actually resolved, and that all information required to describe the incident's lifecycle is supplied in sufficient detail. In addition, the findings from the resolution of the incident are to be recorded for future use.

Proactive user information: This process will inform users of service failures as soon as these are known to the service desk, so that users are in a position to adjust themselves to interruptions. Proactive user information also aims to reduce the number of enquiries by users. This process is also responsible for distributing other information to users, e.g. security alerts.

Incident management reporting: This process will supply incident-related information to other service management processes and ensure that improvement potentials are derived from past incidents.

CHAPTER 6: PROBLEM MANAGEMENT

'I have yet to see any problem, however complicated, which, when you looked at in the right way, did not become still more complicated.'

Paul Anderson

What is a problem?

A problem is an incident, or multiple incidents, for which the root cause is not known. Problems can sometimes be discovered because of multiple incidents exhibiting similar systems, e.g. a computer not booting-up occasionally is an incident but the same computer (or all similar models) not booting-up every Monday morning is a problem that needs further investigation. Until a solution is found, those end-users will face the same issues week after week. An incident cannot be classified as a problem because of the end-user's seniority, or the tantrums end-users may throw. For example, if the mouse of the CEO's computer is not working, it is still an incident, and will not be called a problem simply because of his seniority or power. However, the incident may get a higher priority based on prior service level agreements.

The ITIL definition of a problem is:

'A cause of one or more incidents. The cause is not usually known at the time a problem record is created, and the problem management process is responsible for further investigation.'

What is problem management?

Problem management is part of the service operation phase of the core lifecycle. This is a process that investigates and identifies the root causes of incidents. Effective problem management halts the recurrence of incidents. The goal of problem management is to minimise the adverse impact of incidents and problems on the business that are caused by errors within the IT infrastructure. Failure to halt the recurrence of incidents leads to lost time and frustrated users. Problem management has both proactive and reactive roles. In proactive roles they identify and solve problems before incidents start occurring. An example of a proactive role is to inform all tech staff to apply a video driver update, on all computers, to prevent potential monitor failures, by reading about the potential trouble on the video manufacturer's website. In a reactive role, they identify and solve problems after incidents start appearing, informing all the tech staff to apply a video driver update, on all computers, after noticing several monitors are failing due to a video driver fault.

The ITIL definition of problem management is:

'The process responsible for managing the lifecycle of all problems. The primary objectives of problem management are to prevent incidents from happening, and to minimise the impact of incidents that cannot be prevented.'

Why is problem management necessary?

As mentioned in the previous chapter, an incident management team attends computer issues and fixes them as soon as possible. However, this is not the long-term solution. An incident management team cannot, and should not, keep attending and fixing the same type of computer, and other IT troubles every day. It is necessary to investigate and research why such troubles are occurring in the first place. This is where problem management will help. A problem management team is that specialist department whose main responsibility is to identify permanent solutions to various types of IT troubles in an organisation.

Table 5: Examples of incidents and problems

Incidents	Problems
A computer not booting-up once	Several computers not booting-up periodically
A web server crashing occasionally	A web server crashing every time the user connections hit 60%
One computer freezing-up when a word processor is launched	A set of computers of the identical model freezing when a word processor is launched
An occasional data corruption in a server	Frequent data corruption on a server, or on many servers

What are the responsibilities of problem management?

The main responsibilities of the problem management department are:

- Problem control
- Error control
- Proactive prevention of problems
- Identifying trends
- Management reports
- Major problem reviews.

What are the sub-processes of problem management?

Problem management has the following sub-processes.

Proactive problem identification: This process will improve overall availability of services by proactively identifying and solving problems, or providing suitable workarounds before further incidents recur. For example, the problem management team can make it mandatory for every computer in the organisation to update anti-virus and necessary software patches, such as service packs, periodically. This will proactively prevent new virus attacks or system failures due to manufacturing bugs.

Problem categorisation and prioritisation: This process will record and prioritise the problem with appropriate diligence, in order to facilitate a swift and effective resolution.

Problem diagnosis and resolution: This process will identify the underlying root cause of a problem and initiate the most appropriate and economical problem solution. If possible, a temporary workaround is supplied. For example, by studying the incidents of web server failures over a few weeks, it may be possible to discover a pattern that shows servers failing whenever the load crosses more than 200 connections. This can then be investigated further, and a proper fix or upgrade initiated.

Problem and error control: This process will constantly monitor outstanding problems with regard to their processing status, so that where necessary, corrective measures may be introduced.

Problem closure and evaluation: This process will ensure that after every successful problem solution, the problem record contains a full historical description, and that related, known error records are updated.

Major problem review: This process will review the resolution of a problem in order to prevent recurrence and learn any lessons for the future. Furthermore, it is to be verified whether the problems marked as closed have actually been eliminated. After discovering or resolving any major problem in the infrastructure, the problem management team should conduct detailed reviews. These reviews should discuss and document what went right, what went wrong, why, what could have been done better and how to prevent it from occurring. This is also sometimes known as PIR (post-implementation review).

Problem management reporting: This process aims to ensure that the other service management processes, as well as IT management, are informed of outstanding problems, their processing-status and existing workarounds. It involves the generation of required reports for management. For example, the management may want to know the major list of unresolved problems, how many times their main server has failed over a period of three months, or how many times their network has been attacked by viruses, causing loss of data. It should be possible to present reports required by the business to study and take necessary precautions. For example, the sales and business staff of RockSolid Corp cannot commit to their external customers that all air conditioner purchase orders will be processed within 48 hours, if they discover that their purchase and invoicing computer system is usually down for several days in a month.

What is a known error database?

This is an orderly list of all incidents for which solutions, root causes and workarounds are available and documented. The database contains solutions of all internal, and possibly some external, known errors. It is like a solutions dictionary.

The ITIL definition of a known error database is

'A database containing all known error records. This database is created by problem management and used by incident and problem management. The known error database may be part of the configuration management system, or may be stored elsewhere in the service knowledge management system.'

An entry in a known error database could be:

Error code 45: If a computer pops an error code 45 when trying to access a mail server, then installing a software patch, called ABC, can rectify the error.

Service desk or incident management personnel can have access to a known error database, to provide solutions to end-users immediately. Most help desk software also provides a knowledge base option that can be used as a known error database. A known error database need not be a bells-and-whistles software program. It can just be a good spreadsheet that has all the errors and solutions documented and which is maintained properly by the respective IT departments.

Examples of management reports

Management reports can vary from organisation to organisation in terms of detail and type of reports. However, all management reports have to provide information about how well, or poorly, the organisation's IT systems and services are working, and how they are affecting the business. Managers will usually be interested in how IT services are affecting their financial loss or gain. Table 6 shows a typical example of a problem management status report.

Table 6: A typical problem management status report

Sl no.	Problem	Status	Remarks
1	RockSolid web server hanging when more than 200 users access it.	Resolved	Problem solved by applying a software patch.
2	Unable to install latest e-mail client on all 35 IBM computers purchased last year.	Under investigation	To use old version of client until solution is found. Vendor to provide a solution.
3	Finance servers frequently locking up. Data loss due to abnormal reboots.	Under investigation	No solution yet. Coordinating with vendor to find a solution.

Example: Problem management investigating an issue

Problem Manager: 'Hello, CBZ Software Company. My name is Tim from RockSolid Corp. We have a peculiar issue of all our finance servers locking up frequently, especially every Monday. We are losing valuable data. The only software that is installed on those servers is your finance package Version 7. Would you have any idea what is happening?'

CBZ Tech Support: 'Hello, Tim? Did you say you are running Version 7 on those servers? That software version has a bug which causes servers to lock-up and corrupt data when its connections exceed 200. You will have to upgrade to Version 8 to solve the bug. Please check our website for further details.'

Problem Manager: 'Thanks. We'll have a look and get back to you.'

CHAPTER 7: CHANGE MANAGEMENT

'Everyone thinks of changing the world, but no one thinks of changing himself.'

Leo Tolstoy

What is change?

Today, technology and related business models are transforming at an alarming rate. Organisations have to adopt the latest technologies and processes rapidly, to be competitive and innovative to their clients. In IT, changes usually mean implementing new hardware, software, network equipment, a tool or an upgrade. In ITIL, a change is any addition, deletion, modification, etc. that affects IT. Upgrading a payroll software version on an important finance server is a change. However, change should not be implemented just for the sake of speed, or in a haphazard manner. An orderly and careful process is required for implementing change, based on business requirements, security, etc. Any business process upgrades are likely to require significant technological changes. Thus the IT group must be geared up to adopt and implement change, as and when the business requires it. Good change management will ensure that the business is not put at unwanted risk by implementing changes in a haphazard manner.

The ITIL definition of change is:

'The addition, modification or removal of anything that could have an effect on IT services. The scope should include changes to all architectures, processes, tools, metrics and documentation, as well as changes to IT services and other configuration items.'

What is change management?

Change management is part of the service transition phase of the ITSM core lifecycle. Change management is a process responsible for controlling and managing changes to the IT infrastructure or services, and minimising any risk of disruption to the business. The change management function is responsible for managing change in an IT environment. Some key goals of the change management process are to ensure that all parties affected by a given change are aware, and understand the impact, of the proposed change. Since most IT systems are heavily interrelated, any changes made in one part of a system may have a profound impact on another. Change management attempts to identify all affected systems and processes before the change is implemented, in order to mitigate or eliminate any adverse effects. IT services should not allow any techie to simply upgrade a software version on a main production server, without change management reviewing and approving it. The change management team must first study the need for the upgrade, the benefits it will offer, the risks and downtime associated with the change and how to back out if something goes wrong, before approving the change.

The ITIL definition of change management is:

'The process responsible for controlling the lifecycle of all changes. The primary objective of change management is to enable beneficial changes to be made, with minimum disruption to IT services.'

Why is change management important?

Many may view change management as a bothersome process, but it is extremely important to have an orderly change implementation, to minimise any business risk of haphazard changes. It has been observed that applying changes improperly, or with brazen confidence, is the root cause of a large number of IT infrastructure issues. For example, a techie may confidently apply a software patch on a main server, hoping to solve a bug without involving change management, but later that patch could cause some finance software running on that server to go haywire, resulting in severe issues for the finance department. If the organisation had a proper change management process, they could have studied the proposed change, its impact on the server and end-users, and demanded a back-out plan and a testing plan which could have avoided the crisis. If there was no change management, it would be possible for end-users and techies in the organisation to install whatever software they wanted, or to change settings without knowing the business and licensing implications and security aspects. For example, a techie could upgrade an anti-virus program running on a server because the previous version was causing the server to be slow; or a techie could change a software setting on an important mail server to fix some minor trouble and end up disabling the access to all users, due to a bug. Such uncontrolled or brazen changes can make the whole network compromised, crippled, or go out of control. There has to be some law and order when implementing changes on critical systems, even if they are just minor changes.

Figures 6 and *7* illustrate the differences between IT infrastructures without, and with, change management.

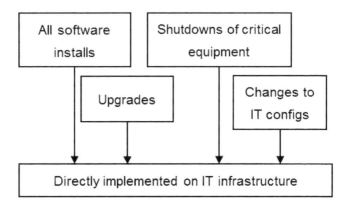

Figure 6: Without change management

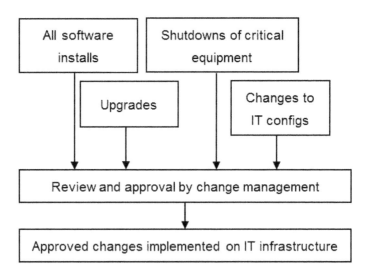

Figure 7: With change management

What are the responsibilities of change management?

An important goal of the change management process is to ensure that standardised methods and procedures are used to handle all changes. Some of the main responsibilities of change management are:

- Accepting, recording and filtering RFCs (requests for change).

- Assessing impact on the business.

- Prioritising changes.

- Justifying, approving and rejecting changes.

- Chairing the CAB (Change Advisory Board) and the CAB/Emergency committee.

- Managing and coordinating implementation.

- Closing RFCs.

- Reporting.

A fuller explanation of each of these is as follows:

Accepting, recording and filtering RFCs: The change management team may get several requests for change. These requests will have to be recorded, registered and an identification number assigned for each. This should also categorise the changes into proper IT areas and priorities. A broad classification could be RFCs for software upgrades or RFCs for hardware upgrades. A sub-classification could be urgent, medium and routine changes.

Assessing impact on the business: Here, the change management team must study each request in detail, to see how it will affect the business. RFCs can be classified as having a minimum, medium or major impact on the business. Certain changes, such as the addition of a new server, may not have a significant impact on the business, but other changes, such as upgrading the operating system on a production server, may have a big impact. Necessary decisions, including rejection, will have to be taken depending on the impact and costs associated with the change.

Prioritising changes: Requested changes must be assigned a priority. Obviously, every change cannot have the same priority. Some changes will be urgent, some will be routine and some will be immediate. For example, a memory upgrade on a few machines may take a lower priority than an emergency anti-virus update on all machines. Prioritising changes can also decide when the change can be applied. It may specify that all hardware upgrades must be carried out after business hours, to minimise downtime.

Justifying, approving and rejecting changes: The change management team will have the authority to justify, approve or reject RFCs, based on various factors. An unnecessary change, such as installing a newer version of a word processor on all machines, may be rejected because the business has no use for it. In another case, the team may justify the expense and implementation of a new version of anti-virus software because it will protect the business against several new viruses.

Chairing the Change Advisory Board (CAB) and the CAB/Emergency committee: A CAB is a group of people who are responsible for assessing, from a business and a technical viewpoint, all high-impact RFCs. They advise change management on the priorities of RFCs, and propose allocations of resources to implement those changes.

A CAB will usually consist of senior members from SLM (service level management – covered in *Chapter 10*), problem management, finance, business managers and technical specialists. It may also include external and third-party members (for example, a consultant from ABC-Telecom) if required. A change manager chairs the CAB, which can meet regularly, or as and when required. When major problems arise, it may not be possible to assemble the full CAB and go through all the bureaucratic formalities. It is therefore necessary to have a smaller, rapid action team, with the necessary authority, called the emergency committee, to take urgent decisions. This team can also take decisions over the phone, depending on the criticality.

Managing and coordinating implementation: The change management team is only responsible for managing changes. It is a consulting and approving body and is not responsible for implementing changes. Implementing changes will be the responsibility of the respective departments, such as release management (covered in Chapter 8).

Closing RFCs: After a change has been approved and all essential activities have been performed, the RFC will have to be closed.

Reporting: This will involve generating the necessary reports for the management. This can evaluate how the change was applied, what issues were faced, were there any unforeseen troubles, etc.

What will an RFC usually consist of?

An RFC is a proposal for change to any component of an IT infrastructure or an IT service. It can be a form that outlines the change requested and the person requesting the change enters all relevant details. It is better to enter as many details as possible. The standard components of an RFC are as follows:

- RFC identification number
- Date requested
- Person requesting the change (with contact details)
- Reason for change
- CI current and proposed change details
- The issue (this can be a recurring incident, problem or a necessary upgrade)
- Details of change proposed (why, when, where)
- Cost details (if available)
- Business impact (high, medium, low)
- Risks (if any)
- How it will be implemented
- Back-out plan, or workaround, if something goes wrong
- Personnel, external vendors, required
- When the change will be required
- Other relevant details.

In addition to these, a completed RFC will contain comments and remarks entered by the CAB and other authorised persons.

It may also contain details, such as:

- Status (approved, rejected, deferred)

- Request for additional details

- Dates for implementation.

For example, the CAB can have an RFC for upgrade of the anti-virus software on all computers, and an RFC for upgrade of a word processor. The CAB may approve the anti-virus upgrade and defer the word processor upgrade because virus prevention is more important than upgrading a word processor.

Is RFC and CAB approval required for every change?

Not exactly. The change management team will get involved only for certain types of change. Other regular changes can be given a single approval. For example, the CAB may give a permanent ongoing approval for weekly anti-virus updates on all servers, without calling for a meeting and preparing RFCs.

Examples of change management reports

Depending on the size of the organisation and the number of changes requested, various types of reports can be prepared.

Some of the common ones are:

- Total number of changes requested this month, this quarter, by department

- Number of changes, classified by priority

- Number of changes approved

- Number of changes deferred or rejected

- Number of successful changes

- Number of changes that required back-out.

Example: A simple RFC

RFC number: Prod-32-2004.

Requested by: Tim of problem management team.

Change requested: Upgrade of finance package from Version 7 to Version 8.

Reason: Version 7 has a bug that causes servers to freeze frequently when connections exceed 200. Requires a reboot to restore connections. There is also loss of financial data every time the machines are booted. Vendor recommends upgrade to solve problem. Details and vendor recommendations attached.

Details of CIs: CI-1 to CI-6 (All finance department servers).

Cost details: £1,000 per server. Total Cost £6,000.

Business impact: High. Must be done as soon as possible.

Back-out plan: Release to be done only on a weekend. Complete back-up of data to be carried out prior to upgrade. Vendor to assist in upgrade and back-out if upgrade fails.

Personnel required: Release management, vendor and persons from the finance department.

Change required by when: Urgent. As soon as possible.

Other details: Upgrade to be purchased from vendor. Delivery period: two weeks.

Status: Approved.

What are the sub-processes of change management?

Change management has the following sub-processes.

Change management support: This process will provide templates and guidance for the authorisation of changes, and supply the other IT service management processes with information on planned and ongoing changes.

Assessment of change proposals: This process will assess change proposals that are submitted for implementing changes by service strategy. The purpose of assessing change proposals is to identify possible issues before the start of design activities.

RFC logging and review: This process will filter out requests for change which do not contain all information required for assessment, or which may seem impractical or unnecessary.

Assessment and implementation of emergency changes: This process will assess, authorise and implement an emergency change as quickly as possible. This process is invoked if normal change management procedures cannot be applied because some emergency requires immediate action.

Change assessment by the change manager: This process will determine the required level of authorisation for the assessment of a proposed change. Major changes are passed on to the CAB for assessment, while minor changes are immediately assessed and authorised by the change manager.

Change assessment by the CAB: This process will assess a proposed change and authorise the change planning phase. If required, higher levels of authority (e.g. IT management) are involved in the authorisation process.

Change scheduling and build authorisation: This process will authorise detailed change and release planning, and assess the resulting project plan prior to authorising the change build phase.

Change deployment authorisation: This process will assess if all required change components have been built and properly tested, and authorise the change deployment phase.

Minor change deployment: This process will implement low-risk, well-understood changes which do not require the involvement of release management.

Post implementation review and change closure: This process will assess the course of the change implementation and the achieved results, in order to verify that a complete history of activities is present for future reference, and to make sure that any mistakes are analysed, and lessons learned.

CHAPTER 8: RELEASE AND DEPLOYMENT MANAGEMENT

'Probably the only place where a man can feel really secure is in a maximum security prison, except for the imminent threat of release.'

Germaine Greer

What is a release?

A release is an authorised and tested change to the IT infrastructure or service. A set of new files that upgrade an anti-virus program from Version 1 to Version 2 can be called a release. A techie may view this as a bunch of files to be copied from a DVD into a production file server, but, from the ITIL perspective, it is a release because the change management team has approved copying of the files to the specified file server.

The ITIL definition of a release is:

'One or more changes to an IT service that are built, tested and deployed together. A single release may include changes to hardware, software, documentation, processes and other components.'

What is release management?

Release management is part of the service transition phase of the ITSM core lifecycle. Any modern IT infrastructure will consist of hardware, software, configuration settings and operational methodologies. There could be several interdependencies that could cripple the entire network if not properly managed. Applying a software patch on a server without properly evaluating it in a separate test environment, or without knowing how to roll back, may cause the server to go haywire if the patch has a bug. Change management ensures that no changes are made to the IT infrastructure or services without going through the necessary approvals. The release management team is responsible for the release and distribution of software into the live environment, coordinating the implementation and for secure storage of authorised IT equipment and software. For example, release management will provide the necessary files, CD-ROM, or a package to be installed on five specific servers if (and only if) change management has authorised them.

The ITIL definition of release management is:

'The process responsible for planning, scheduling and controlling the movement of releases to test and live environments. The primary objective of release management is to ensure that the integrity of the live environment is protected and that the correct components are released. Release management is part of the release and deployment management process.'

What is a deployment?

The ITIL definition of a deployment is:

'The activity responsible for movement of new or changed hardware, software, documentation, process, etc. to the live environment. Deployment is part of the release and deployment management process.'

What is release and deployment management?

It is the process responsible for both release management and deployment (R&D). Release and deployment management is part of the service transition phase of the core lifecycle.

The ITIL definition of the release and deployment process is:

'The process responsible for planning, scheduling and controlling the build, test and deployment of releases, and for delivering new functionality required by the business, while protecting the integrity of existing services.'

Why should there be a R&D management team?

As mentioned earlier, a modern IT infrastructure may consist of hundreds of machines and dozens of software programs and network equipment. All these will have to work properly for the business to run its operations. A release management team ensures safety while installing updates and upgrades. For example, the CAB may have approved the upgrade of an e-mail server from Version A to Version B. However, it is the release management's responsibility to create a CD-ROM, or a set of files, that will do the upgrade. They will also ensure that they have a mechanism to roll the server back to Version A if something goes wrong with the upgrade. If there is no release management to study the release and rollback properly, changes may not be successful, or may even result in various troubles after the upgrade. It is absolutely necessary to have an orderly and controlled method of implementing changes to the IT infrastructure, and this is where the release management team will help. A poorly designed release and deployment management will force IT staff to spend lots of time troubleshooting and managing complexity, or downtime, later. At worst it can degrade and cripple services.

What are the responsibilities of R&D management?

The goal of release and deployment management is to ensure that all technical and non-technical aspects of a release are carried out in an orderly manner that will ensure a successful change, or a rollback if there is some trouble. The release and deployment management personnel deploy releases into production, and enable effective use of the service in order to deliver value.

They have a number of responsibilities:

- Prepare comprehensive release and deployment plans, prepare release policies, documents and procedures.

- Release acceptance, plan roll-out, sign-off, etc.

- Implement, or oversee, implementation of new software and hardware into the operational environment.

- Testing and building releases. Improved consistency in implementation approaches across the business change and service teams. Build release packages, test and deploy efficiently to the target environment.

- Storage of hardware, software and associated inventory (called DML – covered in *Chapter 8*).

- Ensure there is minimal impact on the production services, operations and support. Customers and users are satisfied with the service transition practices and outputs.

- Ensure that the configuration management database (CMDB – covered in *Chapter 9*) is updated.

- Withdrawal of services.

A fuller explanation of some of these is as follows:

Prepare release policies, documents and procedures: This will involve preparing the necessary rules and regulations for releases.

A typical rule for releases might be as follows: '*All software and hardware upgrades of any nature, on any production servers, must be completed only after business hours, after ensuring that two complete image back-ups are taken.*'

Release acceptance, plan roll-out and sign-off: After a change has been approved, the release management team will study the changes and accept them for roll-out. It may even reject them based on technical or workload constraints, or it may request more information and resources. After acceptance, the release team will have to plan how to roll out, depending on the nature of the change.

Testing and building releases: This will involve testing the changes in a separate test environment, to study how the changes will behave in, or affect, the production environment. Building a release may involve additional work, such as creating a self-installable software package from the original vendor-supplied software, for easy deployment. This may involve help from other IT departments or external vendors.

Implement new hardware and software: This means getting the changes installed into the live environment. After testing and certifying that the change will not adversely impact the infrastructure or services, it will have to be implemented at agreed times.

Storage of software and hardware: The release management team is also responsible for the safe storage of all software, hardware and other authorised IT equipment. In ITIL, we use the terms 'definitive software library' (DSL) and 'definitive hardware library' (DHL). A DSL is a collection of all software, CIs and documentation in a secure location. A DSL is a logical library, which means that even though the company may own 50 boxes of Microsoft®

Office® CD-ROMs, the DSL will list them as only one entity called Microsoft® Office®. Physically, a DSL may be a collection of disks, CD-ROMs, tapes, manuals and documents. A simple DSL for RockSolid Corp is show in Table 7.

Table 7: A Simple DSL

Item	Media	Location
Microsoft® Office®	CD-ROM	Firesafe-1
WinZip Version 15.0	Removable media, e.g. a USB stick	Firesafe-1
Windows 8	CD-ROM	Firesafe-1

Similarly, a DHL is a secure storage for hardware items and spares, as shown in Table 8.

Table 8: A Simple DHL

Item	Type	Quantity in store	Quantity distributed
Dell computers	Computer	30	200
IBM computers	Computer	10	250
Spare keyboards	Hardware	5	15

Important note

In ITIL, the concept of DSL is no longer used. Instead, we have a DML, a definitive media library. Similarly, a DHL is also no longer used. However, a DHL is just a secure store facility for all the IT-related hardware and equipment.

What is a DML?

A DML (definitive media library) is one or more locations in which the definitive and approved versions of all software CIs (Configuration Items – explained in *Chapter 9*) are securely stored. The DML may also contain associated CIs, such as licences and documentation. The DML is a single, logical storage area, even if there are multiple locations. All software in the DML is under the control of change and release management, and is recorded in the configuration management system. Only software from the DML is acceptable for use in a release.

What is release building?

It is often necessary to install a piece of software on a number of machines, or it may be necessary to distribute hundreds of machines to end-users within a short time-frame. It may not be possible for the techies to go to every machine and install the necessary software and tools on each, so it is necessary to be able to build a release with the necessary configuration settings, and deploy that build through software deployment tools, or use a centralised location to distribute them. This will ensure that each and every machine receives all the updates in the necessary order. Some examples of building releases are listed below.

Example: Software installation

Assume that a piece of software, such as WinZip, needs to be installed on 100 machines. The traditional method would be to run the set-up from the manufacturer's CD-ROM on each and every machine, enter all the configuration settings (e.g. install location, features required, etc.) and then complete the installation. This method could take a long time and would also be prone to errors. Instead, the WinZip software can be built as a self-installable package with a single executable (e.g. an .msi file) containing all configuration settings built in. This single file can be copied to a central server to which every user has access. As soon as the end-user double-clicks on the msi file, it will install WinZip on his or her machine without any user intervention. Similarly, other software and patches can be deployed like this. This, of course, assumes that the company has purchased 100 WinZip licences.

Example: Hardware deployment

Assume that it is necessary to distribute 200 machines to various end-users. As per standard end-user requirements, each machine must have the operating system, the required service packs, licensed office applications, anti-virus and common tools. If these machines had to be built one by one, it would take a very long time to complete the installation of all machines. Instead, the release management team can build one machine completely, configure all the settings, and then take a snapshot of the complete disk image. This disk image can then be copied to the remaining 199 machines. This will ensure that all 200 machines will be identical in all respects. The machines can then be physically shipped to various end-users who can start using them immediately.

What are the different types of releases?

A release can be of different types based on the software (or hardware) being deployed. The various types of release are:

- Full release

- Delta release

- Package release

- Emergency release.

A fuller explanation of each is as follows:

Full release: Implementation and deployment of all components of a release, e.g. installing a new version of Microsoft® Office® on all computers. In a full release, computers that already have a previous version will get the complete new version in full; computers that did not have a previous version will also get the complete new version installed.

Delta release: Here, the release does not replace all components, but rather includes only those components that have changed since the last release of the software. This is also called partial release. Assume that the full release of Microsoft® Office® was carried out in January, to all computers. In February, the vendor may supply a few DLLs and executables to be installed as a minor patch for Microsoft® Word®. A delta release will package and install only those DLLs and executables to all computers.

Package release: Sometimes it becomes necessary to combine a full and a delta release as a single release. This will be called a package release. A package can be a full base-pack release of anti-virus software, plus the delta release of the latest virus definitions.

Emergency release: (Also called emergency change.) This is usually carried out when there is an urgent need to deploy a release. This is usually to protect the IT infrastructure from a serious risk, or from degradation of an important service. For example, if the company website is being hacked because the server does not have a certain software patch, then it is necessary to take a risk and apply the patch immediately as an emergency release, without too many hurdles.

What is transition planning and support?

Transition planning and support plans and coordinates the resources to move a new or changed service into production within the predicted cost, quality and time estimates. This is not really a new process, as such activities were covered earlier through release and change management. What is new now, is that the transition planning and support process gives this process a high visibility, as it provides guidance for establishing release policies, transition strategies, planning individual service transitions and support for those transitions. It also guides the deployment of new or changed services into the infrastructure.

The ITIL definition is as follows:

'The process responsible for planning all service transition processes and coordinating the resources that they require.'

What is service validation and testing?

In large organisations with multiple changes and releases, it is not possible for a single department to be responsible for everything with a release. A team may create a release package and then hand it over to a testing department to do an elaborate test, under different conditions. The job of the testing department will be to simulate and test the release under different conditions, and to then inform the release department if they notice any issues. In order to do this, an effective build and test environment is essential to ensure the builds and tests are executed in a repeatable and predictable manner. Dedicated build and test environments, such as a lab, must be established for assembling and building components and testing deployments. Test environments must be actively maintained to approximate the conditions of the production environment, to simulate what may happen during releases. The ITIL definition is:

'The process responsible for validation and testing of a new or changed IT service. Service validation and testing ensures that the IT service matches its design specification and will meet the needs of the business.'

What is meant by withdrawal of service?

As the IT infrastructure grows in an organisation, it becomes necessary to implement more and more of the latest tools and equipment. This will also mean that certain old, or outdated, equipment and tools will have to be decommissioned and support stopped. If the entire network has migrated to Windows® 7, then it will be necessary to remove all machines which are running older operating systems, such as NT and Windows® 2000. Even withdrawals of services have to be done in an orderly manner. It is quite possible that some important application could still be running on an old machine. Just because a computer is old, it does not mean you can simply discard it like an electrical appliance, such as a table fan. The old computer could still be running some important application used by the marketing department. In all probability, the old application will not run properly on a new computer with a newer operating system. Therefore, an upgrade and data migration from the old system to the new must be carried out before the old computer is dismantled. Also, IT services must ensure that the end-users migrate to new machines and the latest versions of tools, along with the necessary data, before they decommission the old machines.

It may also be necessary for release management to remove some old software installed on various machines. The release management team may design some automatic scripts to remove, or delete, the tool from all identified machines. Alternatively, they could send out an e-mail with the necessary instructions for end-users to remove the software themselves. Support for those machines and applications would then be stopped by incident and other management services. These sorts of activities constitute a *withdrawal of service*. After services have been withdrawn, necessary information must be provided to all relevant departments, for example, the service desk and incident management, so that they are aware of it. If certain services and applications have been withdrawn, then incident and problem management need not provide support to those services and applications.

What are the sub-processes of release management?

Release management has the following sub-processes.

Release management support: This process provides guidelines and support for the deployment of releases.

Release planning: This assigns authorised changes to release packages and defines the scope and content of releases. With this information, the release planning process develops a schedule for building, testing and deploying the release.

Release build: This process will issue all necessary work orders and purchase requests, so that release components are either bought from outside vendors or developed in-house. At the end of this process, all required release components are ready to enter the testing phase.

Release deployment: This process will deploy the release components into the live production environment. It is also responsible for training end-users and operating staff, and circulating information/documentation on the newly deployed release, or the services it supports.

Early life support: This process will resolve operational issues quickly, during an initial period after release deployment, and remove any remaining errors or deficiencies.

Release closure: This process will formally close a release after verifying if activity logs and CMS (configuration management system) contents are up to date.

CHAPTER 9: SERVICE ASSET AND CONFIGURATION MANAGEMENT

'People are definitely a company's greatest asset. It doesn't make any difference whether the product is cars or cosmetics. A company is only as good as the people it keeps.'

Mary Kay Ash

What is a service asset?

An asset is any resource or capability. Assets of a service provider include anything that could contribute to the delivery of a service, and can be one of the following types: management, organisation, process, knowledge, people, information, applications, infrastructure or financial capital. Resources include IT infrastructure, people, budgets and other things that help in delivering an IT service. Capabilities may develop over the years. Service providers must develop distinctive capabilities that can keep the competition at bay. For capabilities to increase, IT departments must continuously train and upgrade themselves to be competitive. In this book we will be mainly concentrating on technical infrastructure assets.

What is configuration management?

Configuration management is the process responsible for maintaining information about configuration items (CIs – explained shortly) required to deliver an IT service, including their relationships. This information is managed throughout the lifecycle of the CI. Service asset and configuration management (SACM) is part of the service transition phase of the core ITSM lifecycle. This process defines and identifies CIs in the IT infrastructure with their status and other relevant details. Configuration management allows IT departments to have a complete picture of all hardware, software, documentation, versions, locations, relationships and status that exist in their organisation. It allows the identification, control and tracking of all the different versions of hardware, software, documentation, processes, procedures and all other components of the IT environment under the control of change management. The goal of configuration management is to ensure that only authorised components – CIs – are used in the IT environment, and that all changes to them are recorded and tracked correctly.

Is configuration management the same as managing IT inventory?

Not exactly. Configuration management is related to, but different from, inventory or asset management. Configuration management is often confused with asset management, which is a finance department process that includes depreciation and cost accounting. Inventory management systems only maintain details of assets (such as laptops and desktops) above a certain value, their business unit, the purchase price and their location. In general, an asset can be anything the organisation owns – buildings, chairs, tables, computers, etc. There may be no relationships between assets. Configuration management records IT asset details *plus the relationships* between them. Configuration management will also deal with items that are not usually found in an asset register, such as documentation for Server A. The important feature of configuration management is that it documents relationships between CIs. For example,

Server A (CI) used by the sales department is connected to LAN Switch 2 (CI) connected to UPS-B (CI), and the documentation (CI) of Server A is available on 16 (CI) stored in Fire safe 12 (CI). Configuration management will rely on a CMDB (configuration management database – explained shortly) to store the information required. Inventory or asset management will depend on an asset register, or some other tool.

Why is configuration management important?

For any IT infrastructure to be stable, recoverable, able to deploy smooth upgrades and ensure minimum disruption to end-users, it is absolutely necessary to have a complete and correct picture of the entire infrastructure and their interrelationships. The cost of not having a proper configuration of the network or services and their relations, can be very high. Suppose the techies simply upgrade an e-mail software version (CI) on a central server (CI) without knowing that this upgrade also involves upgrading the e-mail client software (CI) on all desktops. The next morning none of the end-users would be able to connect to their e-mail server. This could result in major chaos and the service desk could be inundated with hundreds of support calls, and the other technical teams would not be able to manage such a crisis. However, if the complete configuration of the mail server and its technical relationship to various desktops were known, this crisis could be avoided.

What is service asset and configuration management?

Service asset and configuration management (SACM) is the process responsible for both configuration management and asset management. It aims to maintain information about configuration items required to deliver an IT service, including their relationships.

What is a configuration item?

A configuration item (CI) is any component, or item, or the IT infrastructure, which is under the control of configuration management. Examples of CIs include computers, hardware, software, network equipment, configurations, processes, procedures, telephony equipment, documentation, service level agreements and problem records. CIs can vary widely in complexity, size and type, and can range from entire systems (e.g. a mainframe computer) to minor hardware items (e.g. modems). A production file server, the applications installed on it, the documents about the applications and the disaster recovery plan for the server, would all be individual CIs. The complexity is your choice. You may decide that a computer is a CI, or you may decide to break into its components (CPU, keyboard, mouse and monitor), and make each of these a CI. The CI data controlled by configuration management is stored in the CMDB, which is a relational database used to track CIs in the IT environment.

You should start by defining very high-level CIs. Identifying critical services and their components is also a useful place to start with configuration management.

Examples of critical CIs could be:

- Critical servers, computers and laptops.

- Important LAN switches, routers, data lines, voice lines and telecom equipment.

- List of all important business applications and their documentations.

- All important databases and their connections.

- Standalone devices, such as firewalls, security equipment, modems, scanners, printers, special devices and black boxes.

- Important documents for the above.

What is a CI attribute?

A dictionary defines 'attribute' as a quality or characteristic inherent to someone or something. In ITIL, a CI attribute means the description of a CI, such as make/model number, version number, supplier, purchase order, contract number, release number, date installed and relationships held in the CMDB. Attributes describe the characteristics of a configuration item that are valuable, and necessary, for recording. Infrastructure items are expensive and valuable to every organisation. It is necessary to record as many important details of an infrastructure item as possible for its maintenance, support and finally its disposal.

Some of the necessary attributes of a CI are:

- **CI name:** This is an identifiable name given to a CI. This will have to be unique among all CIs. Two file servers should not be called FS-1. They can be FS-1 and FS-2.

- **Serial numbers, models, licence and version number:** These can be the item's serial number and name provided by the manufacturer, e.g. Compaq Presario 500 Series, or a software name with a licence number.

- **Category:** CIs will have to be properly classified into various categories, such as hardware, computers, software, documents and consumables.

- **Details of the equipment:** Dell Server with Pentium processor, 16 GB RAM, 400 GB hard disk, 17 inch monitor and external tape drive.

- **Warranty and maintenance details:** Whether the item is still under warranty, or under maintenance after warranty. If under maintenance, then include details of vendor and contact number.

- **Department details:** Which internal department is using the server, who is the contact, etc.

- **Status:** This can state whether the item is a live production CI, test or standby equipment.

A simple configuration item detail, in this case of a particular file server, is shown in *Table 9*. In this, multiple CIs (hardware, software, etc.) are all clubbed under a single CI for easy maintenance.

Table 9: Details for file server ENG-FS-1

CI details	
Server Name	ENG-FS-1 (IBM Pentium 4, 2 GB RAM, 50 GB disk)
IP Address	170.30.2.1
Physical Location	3rd Floor, Room 7
Serial Number	QW34T7
ID Number or Asset Tag	SERVER-54
Status	Production
Operating System	Windows 2008 with Service Pack 1
Connection	To main Cisco® switch
Anti-Virus	McAfee Ver-10
Software-1	AutoCAD Ver-4
Software-2	Corel Draw Ver-10 with Service Pack 2
Maintained by	IBM, Ph: 988 8675
Documents	Stored in same server DOCS Directory on C: Drive
Business Contact	Mr Anderson, Ph: 765 4321
Users	All engineering staff on 5th floor
Last upgrade	10 July 2014
Signature	

What is a CI relationship?

In any IT infrastructure, the various CIs cannot work in isolation or independently of each other. For example, a piece of software must be installed on a computer for it to be used. This forms a simple *relationship* between two CIs, the computer and the software. The CMDB should show that this software is installed on a particular computer and is being used by a particular department. There can also be a complex relationship among several CIs. A central sales database server could have several different programs and tools installed on it. All the hardware, software, tools, documents, departments using the server, etc. will form a complex relationship, which has to be captured in the CMDB.

What is the configuration management database?

The configuration management database (CMDB) is a database containing details of all CIs and the relationships between them. Depending on the organisation's size, a CMDB can vary from a small tool to capture such information, to a complex, asset management system that can hold a global view of all IT assets and their relationships. The database information can be held in a variety of formats, such as a diagram of the entire network, with a text description of each CI.

The ITIL definition of a CMDB is:

'A database used to store configuration records throughout their lifecycle. The Configuration Management System (CMS) maintains one or more CMDBs, and each CMDB stores attributes of CIs, and relationships with other CIs.'

A very simple picture of a CMDB (*see Figure 8*) could show file server ENG-FS1 providing access to AutoCAD Version 4.0 drawing software to 15 design workstations running in the engineering department. The relationship here is that those 15 design workstations (CIs) depend on the file server (CI) and Cisco® switch (CI) for their work. Any unapproved or unannounced changes to the file server, or the cisco switch, could affect the engineering department end-users.

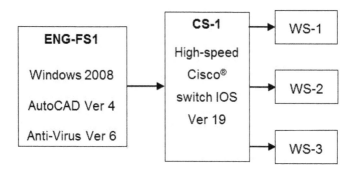

Figure 8: A simple picture of a CMDB

What is a configuration management system?

A configuration management system (CMS) can be viewed as a container, or a beehive, of CMDBs, CIs and other components. A CMS can hold multiple CMDBs. To manage large and complex organisations, SACM uses a CMS. The CMS maintains one or more CMDBs, and each CMDB stores attributes of CIs, and their relationships with other CIs. CMS was introduced in ITIL Version 3 onwards, to remove the common confusion that the CMDB represented just a single database that covers all CIs possible in an organisation. In reality, an organisation may contain multiple CMDBs for various IT departments, and the CMS is a container for all these. The CMS is used for a wide range of purposes, and maintains the relationships between all service components and related incidents, problems and known errors. It may also contain corporate data about employees, suppliers, locations, business units and customers.

The ITIL definition of CMS is:

'A set of tools, data and information that is used to support service asset and configuration management. The CMS is part of an overall service knowledge management system and includes tools for collecting, storing, managing, updating, analysing and presenting data about all configuration items and their relationships. The CMS may also include information about incidents, problems, known errors, changes and releases. The CMS is maintained by service asset and configuration management and is used by all IT service management processes.'

What are the responsibilities of configuration management?

The role of configuration management is important, as it maintains the CMDB. It is very important to maintain an accurate and current CMDB, as other teams – incident, problem, change, release management, etc. – use it extensively. Some of the main responsibilities of configuration management are to:

- Be accountable for all IT assets and configurations within the organisation and its services. Label and record details of equipment.

- Provide accurate and current information on CI configurations, relationships, locations and their documentation, for other departments (e.g. incident management, problem management, change management and release management) to use.

- Verify, and update, the CMDB after changes are implemented, or after withdrawal of services.

- Provide necessary documentation and reporting.

How are CMDBs managed?

In order to manage a CMDB, it must first be created. Depending on the size of the organisation, it can range from a simple, detailed spreadsheet, to using a third-party tool to document and update the various CIs and their relationships. An organisation can also have multiple CMDBs. The network management team can have a CMDB consisting only of LAN switches, routers and modems. The computer support team can have a CMDB consisting of servers, desktops and printers. So, when a change is being implemented, both the teams will have to put their heads together and ensure changes in one do not affect the other. The important thing is to have the CMDB always accurate and current. A vital, initial activity will be deciding which items are to be included in the CMDB. Only important, useful and concise information should be entered. If too many details are entered, the CMDB will soon become unmanageable and cumbersome to update.

Table 10 shows a very simple CMDB and its update after a service pack upgrade with a change of business owner.

Now the various teams can use the latest information for any of their requirements.

Table 10: A simple CMDB with service pack upgrade

CI list	Before update	After update
Server Name	ENG-FS-1	ENG-FS-1
IP Address	170.30.2.1	170.30.2.1
Physical Location	3rd Floor, Room 7	3rd Floor, Room 7
Serial Number	QW34T7	QW34T7
ID Number	SERVER-54	SERVER-54
Status	Production	Production
Operating System	Windows 2003 with Service Pack-3	Windows 2008 with Service Pack-1
Connection	To Main Cisco® Switch	To Main Cisco® Switch
Anti-Virus	McAfee® Ver-10	McAfee® Ver-12
Software-1	AutoCAD® Ver-4	AutoCAD® Ver-6
Software-2	Corel Draw® Ver-10 with Service Pack-2	Corel Draw® Ver-11 with Service Pack-1
Maintained By	IBM, Ph 9888675	IBM, Ph 9888675
Documents	Stored in same server. DOCS directory on C Drive	Stored in same server. DOCS directory on C Drive
Business Contact	Mr Anderson Ph: 7654321	Mr James Ph: 7654377
Last upgrade	10 July 2012	12 Sep 2014
Users	All engineering staff on 5th floor	All engineering staff on 5th floor and 7th floor
Signature		

What is a configuration baseline?

This is a snapshot of a CI, or multiple CIs, at a point in time. A snapshot of a file server with its operating system, various software and data, as at 10 January 2008, is a configuration baseline. The baseline is a reference for future changes. Having a baseline is very important, and will help in back-out if some change release fails to get installed properly. If a Cisco® router has to be upgraded from a firmware Version 10 to Version 11, then the techies can take a back-up of the Cisco® router's configuration and settings before applying Version 11. This will be a baseline for changes. If Version 11 fails to work properly, then they can revert back to Version 10 and all previous settings. If the upgrade was successful, then Version 11 and all its new settings will become the new baseline for future upgrades. Depending on the size of the organisation and IT departments, there can be several baselines. The software support division can maintain a baseline of all software installed in various servers, and the network support division can maintain a baseline of the current routers and switches.

What is a baseline analyser?

Many hardware and software vendors provide network scanning and discovery tools, to find out the versions of hardware, software and network equipment installed in the organisation. These tools can scan an individual PC, or an entire LAN, and find out what is installed and what is missing. Microsoft® provides a network scan tool called Microsoft® Baseline Security Analyzer® that can scan all the machines on the local network, to find out what service packs and hot fixes are installed in each and every machine's Windows operating system. It is not necessary to go to each and every machine to find out what is installed, or what is not. Depending on need, IT services can then decide what to do next.

Example: ITIL jargon

Regular-Techie: 'I have received an order to initiate approved Change Request Number-Prod-32-2004 for CI-Numbers 1 to 6, by ensuring a back-up of the weekend baseline on 30 July 2004, and later send the required version details to Configuration Management to update CMDB. Help! What do I need to do?'

ITIL-Techie: 'Don't worry. It just means that you need to copy all files (Change Prod-32-2004) from this CD-ROM into the D drive's FINANCE directories (D:\FINANCE) of FS-1 to FS-6 (CI Numbers 1 to 6). However, ensure that you take a full back-up (baseline) of all the servers on close of business on 30 July, before you copy the files. This will upgrade the Finance Package from Version 7 to Version 8. After you finish the copy, just call up the change management team and tell them that you have completed the job, for them to make a note of this copy (and update the CMDB).'

What is CMDB updating?

After every major release it is necessary to update the CMDB with details of the changes made. If an e-mail server software was upgraded from Version 5 to Version 6, then the CMDB sheet, or diagram pertaining to that server, must be updated. CMDB updates must be carried out in coordination with the change management and configuration management teams.

CMDB before update

> **E-mail Server, EXG-FS1**
> Mail Software Version 5.0
> Last updated: 10 July 2012
> Updated by: Jim of Release Team
> Verified by Rob of Configuration Team
> Copy sent to David of Change Team

CMDB after update

> **E-mail Server, EXG-FS1**
> Mail Software Version 6.0
> Last updated: 24 Sep 2013
> Updated by: Jim of Release Team
> Verified by Rob of Configuration Team
> Copy sent to David of Change Team

Figure 9: A CMDB before and after updating

There are also many help desk and asset management software packages manufactured according to ITIL guidelines. These programs can have a ready-to-use CMDB for most organisations. However, note that there is no ITIL approved, or authorised, software or hardware, as mentioned earlier.

What is software licensing?

Software licensing is a very critical activity in all organisations today. Without software licensing, organisations can get into serious trouble. The amount of information available regarding software licensing could be a separate book by itself. This will involve keeping track of all licences of all software purchased, and how they are distributed throughout the organisation. Managing software licensing is very, very important from a cost, as well as a legal, perspective. Organisations must ensure that they are fully compliant with the respective software's licensing policy, to avoid trouble with the law. It is illegal to buy a single-user version of some software and have it installed on several systems. Managing licences can become a very cumbersome task if not managed properly from the beginning. Licences can be tracked manually (*see Table 11*), or by using several advanced asset management tools available from external vendors.

Table 11: A simple licence management spreadsheet

Software	Licenses purchased	Licenses distributed	Licenses in stock	Locations
Microsoft® Office®	50	45	5	Sales and marketing department
Payroll software	5	5	0	Finance department
Anti-virus	100	100	0	Every PC

Some tips and advice for service asset and configuration management:

- Ensure every IT asset detail is properly recorded in the CMDB or CMS.

- Keep the CMDB updated and dispose of all unused CIs or IT assets.

- Have a separate department to manage and control software licensing for your organisation.

- Label all IT assets properly.

- Do not interchange equipment and assets from different vendors. If you buy IBM and Acer systems, do not replace a failed IBM keyboard with an Acer one just because you have a spare. Maintain all equipment in its invoiced condition so that you can decommission it properly from a technical and finance perspective.

- Make a diagram of the entire organisation and keep it updated.

- Do not drown yourself with too much detail by recording unnecessary molecular and atomic details of a CI.

What are the sub-processes of configuration management?

Configuration management has the following sub-processes.

Configuration identification: This process defines and maintains the underlying structure of CMS, so that it is able to hold all information on configuration items (CIs). This includes specifying the attributes describing CI types and their sub-components, as well as determining their interrelationships.

Configuration control: This ensures that no configuration items are added or modified without the required authorisation, and that such modifications are adequately recorded in the CMS.

Configuration verification and audit: This involves performing regular checks, ensuring that the information contained in the CMS is an exact representation of the configuration items (CIs) actually installed in the live production environment.

CHAPTER 10: SERVICE LEVEL MANAGEMENT

'The palest ink is better than the most retentive memory.'

Chinese Proverb

What is service level management?

Service level management (SLM) is the process of defining, agreeing, documenting and managing an effective IT service that is expected by the business. SLM covers service level agreements (SLAs), operational level agreements (OLAs), underpinning contracts (UCs) and related activities, such as periodic reviews, updating and deletions, as well as publishing, and making them known to all concerned. The main aim of SLM is to ensure an acceptable quality of the IT services provided, at a cost acceptable to the business, and indirectly to the final external consumers of the company's products. SLM is part of the service design phase of the ITSM core lifecycle.

The ITIL definition of SLM is:

'The process responsible for negotiating achievable service level agreements and ensuring that these are met. It is responsible for ensuring that all IT service management processes, operational level agreements and underpinning contracts are appropriate for the agreed service level targets. Service level management monitors and reports on service levels, holds regular service reviews with customers, and identifies required improvements.'

What is a service level agreement?

A service level agreement (SLA) is a signed contract between a service provider and a customer that defines, in writing, the services provided, the metrics associated with those services, acceptable and unacceptable service levels, and liabilities on the part of the service provider and the customer. If a guaranteed level of service is important for your end-users, then business managers should have a proper, negotiated agreement with the IT departments and the service providers they depend on (such as external vendors). Service levels in ITIL are normally the level of service they provide to their businesses. The key to effective SLM is having a clear and proper SLA.

The ITIL definition of an SLA is:

'An agreement between an IT service provider and a customer. The SLA describes the IT service, documents service level targets, and specifies the responsibilities of the IT service provider and the customer. A single SLA may cover multiple IT services or multiple customers.'

Why should there be an SLA?

As mentioned before, businesses depend heavily on IT services for running their business. Whatever IT services do (or don't do), directly affects the business in terms of revenue, reputation and security. The primary goal of IT services is to align with the business objectives. It is important for the business and IT services to negotiate and have a written agreement, or document, that will outline each other's expectations and responsibilities, including financial aspects. Business managers cannot blame IT services for not fixing frequent incidents and problems in the infrastructure, if they are not willing to release appropriate funds to implement stable computer systems or necessary hardware and software upgrades.

The benefits of an effective SLA are well worth the time and effort you put into developing one. Here are some tips for achieving a good SLA:

• Design the SLA so that it clearly defines the IT department's responsibilities. Business managers who want the best possible service must also be willing to pay the necessary money for implementing all the resources needed to get the service. If you pay peanuts you will only get monkeys.

• Negotiate with the IT department or service provider as to what services are being guaranteed, how they will be measured, the processes they use and the amount of time they require.

• Implement SLA measurement and enforcement tools and processes to ensure that every SLA can be measured and enforced on a continuous basis.

What are the responsibilities of SLM?

Having SLM allows a healthy alignment between the business and IT services. Successful SLM will:

• Establish a service catalogue

• Establish proper SLAs

• Establish OLAs

• Establish UCs (underpinning contracts)

• Ensure necessary management reporting

• Review and provide improvement plans.

A fuller explanation of each is as follows:

Service catalogue: A list of all services, priorities, documentation, availability and key contacts, provided by IT services to the business, or a business unit. It may also include service charges and billing information. A catalogue may specify that IT services are responsible for maintaining all computers, servers, printers and telecommunication facilities in the organisation, but that they are not responsible for photocopiers, shredders, fax machines and air conditioners. The service catalogue must be as detailed as possible. It may also specify costs, such as £50 will be charged for every incident attended after business hours. As new services and IT equipment are added, the service catalogue should be updated, and obsolete ones removed. More details of the service catalogue will be provided in the next chapter.

Example: An IT services department with a service catalogue

End-user: 'Hello help desk. The photocopier isn't working. Can you fix it immediately? While you are here, can you also look at the paper shredder?'

Help desk: 'Sorry, we don't fix photocopiers or shredders. We only fix computers.'

End-user: 'Why not? I thought you fixed everything here.'

Help desk: 'No. Please look at our service catalogue on the intranet.'

SLAs: These can be prepared after consultation with the customer (business), and published on the company intranet for every end-user to view.

A basic SLA applicable to every end-user in the organisation could have the following summary:

- **Service catalogue:** IT services will be responsible for all computers in the organisation connected to the network.

- **Contact number:** IT services can be contacted by dialling 8888 from every telephone.

- **Service hours:** IT services can be contacted by any end-user between 9 am and 5 pm Monday to Friday, excluding weekends and holidays.

- **After-hours support:** Available only for the finance department

- **Response:** IT services will ensure that every incident reported will be attended within half a business day. Resolution of the incident will depend on the nature of the incident. Workarounds will be provided wherever possible.

A detailed sample of an SLA is provided in *Appendix 1*.

OLAs (Operating Level Agreements): Organisations can have several IT departments, such as desktop support, server support, network services and software support. These departments must work in a cooperative manner to resolve various IT issues. For example, the computer support team will not be able to provide a new computer connection to a user, until the network support team provides a working network point. If these two departments do not work in a coordinated fashion, the end-users will suffer. OLAs are agreements between, and within, such IT departments. An

OLA can be viewed as an internal, agreed document between various IT departments in an organisation.

We can have OLAs between the following departments:

- Service desk and second-level support
- Second-level support and third-level support
- Service desk and network support department
- IT services and departments who look after electrical supply within the organisations. If the main UPS fails, then IT services will not be able to do anything until the building's electricians rectify the fault. So, IT services can have an agreement with the electrical department to provide standby power units within agreed time-frames.

UCs (Underpinning Contracts): A UC is an agreement with an external or third-party vendor, or supplier, for services and materials required by IT services. IT services could have an agreement with a desktop spares supplier to supply necessary parts within agreed time-frames, for various desktop hardware faults. If a power supply, or a monitor or a motherboard of a computer fails, then it is the responsibility of the external vendor to repair or replace the defective item within agreed time-frames, as covered in the UC. A UC is absolutely essential to all IT services.

Example: IT services without a UC

Desktop Support: 'Hello. We are calling from RockSolid Corp. One of our main server's power supplies has failed. Can you replace it immediately?'

ABC Company: 'Can you read out the serial number of the

---

server?'

Desktop Support: 'It is QW1246.'

ABC Company: 'Sorry, that server is out of warranty, and also not under any support maintenance agreement, so we will not be able to replace the power supply for free. You will have to buy a new power supply.'

Example: IT services with a UC

Desktop Support: 'Hello. We are calling from RockSolid Corp. One of our main server's power supplies has failed. Can you replace it immediately?'

ABC Company: 'Can you read out the serial number of the server?'

Desktop Support: 'It is QW1246.'

ABC Company: 'Thank you for the details. That server is under our maintenance contract. We will replace the power supply within the next four hours.'

Management reporting: The SLM manager can generate the necessary reports to see how well the SLM processes are working, or not working. These reports will have been generated based on measurements specified in the SLA, OLA and UCs.

Management reports can vary from organisation to organisation in terms of details and type of reports. However, all management reports have to provide information about how well (or poorly) the organisation's IT systems and services are working, and how they are affecting the business. They will usually be interested in how IT services are affecting their financial loss or gain. Some of the reports could be:

Incident response percentage report

What percentages of incidents are being attended by IT services personnel within the agreed SLA? If an SLA has specified that all end-user complaints will be attended (not solved) within three hours of reporting, then a report that shows how many incidents were attended within three hours, and how many could not be attended within three hours, could be of interest to management.

Table 13: Summary report for incident response example

Number of incidents	Attended within three hours	Attended after three hours
10	5	5

Table 14: Raw data report for incident response example

Incident number	Committed SLA (hours)	Actual (hours)	Attended within SLA?
IN-1	3	2	Yes
IN-2	3	4	No
IN-3	3	5	No
IN-4	3	1	Yes
IN-5	3	1	Yes
IN-6	3	7	No
IN-7	3	6	No
IN-8	3	2	Yes

| IN-9 | 3 | 2 | Yes |
| IN-10 | 3 | 6 | No |

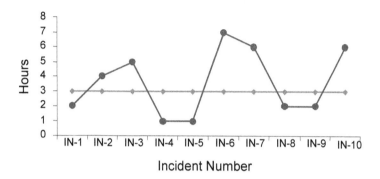

Figure 10: Graphical report for incident response example

This report shows that five of the ten incident support requests have gone out of committed response times (above the horizontal line of three hours). This further means that on average only 50% of the end-users' calls are being attended within agreed times by IT services, whereas the committed percentage was 90% or higher. Hence, nine calls should have been attended within three hours, but only five were. The SLM manager now needs to investigate why there is a gap – maybe IT services have a staff ratio issue or maybe the commitment of 90% was impractical, or IT service personnel may not be properly trained, or equipped, to handle multiple support calls, or perhaps the infrastructure has too many old and outdated systems that often fail.

PO server downtime report

Management may want to know how many times their main purchase order and invoicing system (PO server) was down in a month. A typical report would probably be as shown in *Figure 11*.

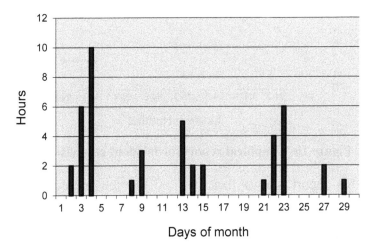

Days of month

Figure 11: Graphical report for PO server downtime example

This report shows that the PO server is frequently down for several hours, on several days of the month. This will directly affect the business, as the sales and delivery department will not be able to meet the organisation's commitment of processing every air conditioner's purchase order within two business days.

The SLM or incident managers, or both, will have to ask the problem management team to investigate why the server is failing so frequently. Maybe the server has a software bug or overload issues. Next they will have to take measures to see that the problem gets reduced after applying the recommendations.

General incidents report

A third type of report could be a generic report, illustrated by Figure 12, showing general incidents for the month of May.

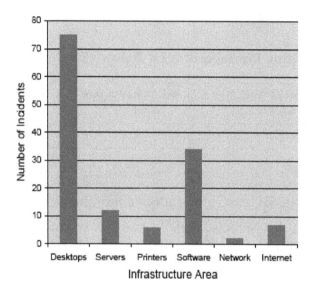

Figure 12: Graphical report for general incidents example

From a business manager's perspective, all the above reports are viewed in terms of revenue loss or gain, or how it affects external customers. Some of the reports show a loss of revenue because many employees in the organisation are not able to do their work because IT services is not attending to, or fixing, the faults within agreed time-frames.

Example: OLA ownership

If an OLA has specified that the second-level support team will take ownership, and resolve, or attend all calls routed to it by the service desk within one business day, then a report can be generated similar to Figure 12.

Table 15: Report for OLA ownership example

Number of incidents assigned	Closed within one day	Closed after one day
35	20	15

Example: UC external vendor commitments

If a UC has specified that the external vendor must provide replacements for all failed computer parts within one business day of registering a service call, then a report can be generated.

Table 16: Report for UC external vendor commitments example

Number of hardware faults logged with vendor	Number of replacements provided within one day	Number of replacements provided after one day
12	4	8

Reviews and improvement plans: After studying various reports generated from month to month, the SLM manager can understand how well the entire SLM is working. If it is noticed that a particular vendor is consistently unable to meet the commitment of supplying spares within agreed time-frames, the manager can find a more effective replacement. Alternatively, if an internal OLA is having some troublesome issues, it has to be sorted out properly between the departments. If second-level support is not responding properly to the calls escalated to them by first-level support, then service levels cannot be met properly. Assume that an end-user has some computer trouble. The first-level techie attends the incident within the committed time and sees that the cause of the trouble is being unable to connect to the network. This may require escalation and assistance from the network support staff, which is second-level support. However, if the second-level support staff do not attend the trouble immediately, then OLAs are not working, and the end-user will not be able to continue working. These issues must be sorted out by involving all concerned, to minimise business impacts.

What are the sub-processes of service level management?

SLM has the following sub-processes.

Maintenance of the SLM framework: This process designs and maintains the underlying structure of the customer agreement portfolio, and provides templates for the various SLM documents.

Identification of service requirements: This process will capture desired outcomes, or requirements, from the customer viewpoint, for new services or major service modifications. The service requirements are to be documented and submitted to an initial evaluation, so that alternatives may be sought at an early stage for requirements which are not technically or economically feasible.

Agreements sign-off and service activation: This involves having all relevant contracts signed off after completion of service transition, and check if service acceptance criteria are fulfilled. In particular, this process makes sure that all relevant OLAs are signed off by their service owners, and that the SLA is signed off by the customer.

Service level monitoring and reporting: This process will monitor achieved service levels and compare them with agreed service level targets. This information is circulated to customers and all other relevant parties, as a basis for measures to improve service quality.

CHAPTER 11: SERVICE CATALOGUE MANAGEMENT

'We used to build civilisations. Now we build shopping malls.'

Bill Bryson

What is a service catalogue?

A general dictionary defines a catalogue as 'a list of titles, course offerings or articles for exhibition or sale, usually including descriptive information or illustrations'. In ITIL language, a service catalogue is a database, or a structured document, containing information about IT services available to current and prospective customers. It can provide a descriptive list of all services a tech support department is responsible for. The catalogue can also contain information about deliverables, prices, contact details, procedures and request processes. By having a service catalogue, organisations can ensure all areas of the business can view an accurate, consistent picture of the IT services, their details, status, and the quality of service the customer can expect from each service. The service catalogue helps to achieve quality of IT services, business and IT alignment, and the control of IT costs.

Need for a catalogue: The purpose of a catalogue is similar to a supermarket catalogue. It provides the following details:

- What services the IT department provides.

- Steps and procedures on how customers can avail of those services.

- Defined boundaries to manage customer expectations and allows the IT department to agree, or reject, to requests that fall outside the range of their defined services.

The service catalogue usually consists of two parts.

1. **Business service catalogue:** The business service catalogue contains details of all the IT services delivered to the customer, including their relationships to the business units and the business processes that rely on them. It provides the customer view of the service catalogue, and is thus more suited for use by business customers and those who need to interface with them.

2. **Technical service catalogue:** This catalogue contains details of all the IT services delivered to the customer, but includes their relationships to the supporting services, shared services, components and configuration items necessary to support them. It is therefore more suited for use by the IT organisation staff to facilitate the management of the services provided, especially since it usually contains details that are not important to business customers. This catalogue does not form part of the customer view and is for use only by the IT department. The technical service catalogue focuses on establishing supporting agreements and contracts (SLAs, OLAs and contracts with external providers).

How do you differentiate the IT service portfolio from the service catalogue?

The service portfolio is composed of all services committed to IT customers, and will contain information on current, under development and future services, as part of continual service improvement. The service catalogue is a subset of the services portfolio that is currently available to IT customers.

What is service catalogue management?

The management of the catalogue consists of the following:

1. Defining the IT service.

2. Creating, publishing and maintaining the catalogue.

3. Ensuring it is current, by adding new or updated services and removing decommissioned services.

4. Agreeing and documenting a service definition with all relevant parties.

5. Agreeing the contents with service portfolio management.

6. Discussing with the business and service continuity management on the dependencies of business units.

7. Interfacing with support teams, suppliers and configuration management for their inputs.

8. Discussing with business relationship management and service level management to ensure the information is aligned to the business.

Why is a service catalogue needed?

Over the years, an organisation's technical infrastructure and IT departments can grow exponentially. Based on business and end-user demands, new equipment will be added and old equipment removed. So, services can expand or shrink in the organisation. However, at any point in time there will be no clear, central picture of all the services being provided by the IT department, or a clear picture available of the customers of each service. Often various employees and business managers will be unaware of what IT services are available to them and what are not (*see example*). This may result in improper requests and duplication in services.

Example: An IT services department without a service catalogue

End-User: 'Hello. . I need to scan a number of documents. Do you know any vendor where I can get it done?'

Help desk: 'No need for a vendor. Why don't you use the common scanning station available on the third floor?'

End-User: 'I didn't know we had a common scanner in our organisation.'

Help desk: 'Oh, we installed that scanner for employees more than six months ago.'

End-User: 'You folks should publish such information on our intranet, or at least shoot a mail to everyone when you install new facilities.'

It is necessary for organisations to have a catalogue outlining what services are available for end-users. A proper service catalogue can help you in the following ways:

- A catalogue of defined IT services puts boundaries on the responsibilities of the IT department. It is a valuable tool in managing customer expectation and allows the IT department to say 'no' to things that fall outside the range of their services. It defines what is *not* provided, as much as what is.

- Management can use the service catalogue to decide the impact, in business terms, of minor and major service

---

> disruptions.
>
> • Once services are properly defined, the process of establishing appropriate service levels and corresponding charges becomes easier.
>
> • Prevents unrealistic expectations from end-users and business managers. Otherwise end-users may assume the IT department can be contacted for anything that uses electricity in the office.

What should a catalogue contain?

When you want to buy something from a website or a company retail catalogue, you have certain basic expectations of what you want to see. Essentially, you expect to find items available for purchase described in simple terms you can understand, along with its full pricing. Without such basic information, you cannot buy anything. The same formula applies to IT departments and their end-users. Unfortunately, it is quite common for end-users to see vaguely defined services from their IT departments without proper details, such as cost and whom to contact. Like a retail catalogue, an IT service catalogue should completely outline all the services the IT department makes available to end-users. In essence, it should be a snapshot of the IT organisation's capability from the customer's perspective.

Table 17 gives an example of a simple, table catalogue that can be published on your intranet, so that end-users can see, at a glance, what IT services areas are available to them in RockSolid Corp.

Additional details about each service can be obtained by clicking in the relevant cell. You can use internal approval methods, such as filling a form or getting an e-mail confirmation, to avail of those services.

Table 17: A simple table catalogue

Main Services	Remarks	Cost	Contact	Add Details
File server services	All LAN users	NA	help@rocksolid.com	click here
Internet service	All LAN users	NA	help@rocksolid.com	click here
E-mail service	All LAN users	NA	help@rocksolid.com	click here
Help desk	All LAN users	NA	help@rocksolid.com	click here
Networking and telecom services	All LAN users	NA	help@rocksolid.com	click here
Word processing; spreadsheets; presentation applications	All LAN users	NA	help@rocksolid.com	click here
Printing and scanning services	All LAN users	NA	help@rocksolid.com	click here
Database and web services	Development project teams only	NA	help@rocksolid.com	click here
Business applications A, B, C and D	Business managers only	NA	help@rocksolid.com	click here
Project management tools	Technical project managers only	NA	help@rocksolid.com	click here

Blackberry services	Senior management only	**£150 pcm**	16H208Hxyz@rocksolid.com	click here
Remote access enabled laptops	Shift operators and after hours support staff only	**NA**	remote@rocksolid.com	click here

The additional details can contain more information of that particular service. If you click the Addl Details button in the networking and telecom services row then it can provide more details of that service, such as:

- **Service catalogue name:** Example: *Catalogue for Networking and Telecom Services.*

- **Date published or updated.**

- **Brief introduction:** Provide a brief introduction for this catalogue. This sub-catalogue will provide networking and telecom services for RockSolid Corp.

- **All services provided:** Provide a list of all individual services, such as Internet services, telephone services, FTP services, voicemail services and new network ports, and the prerequisites to avail them.

- **Service manager:** Contact information (phone, e-mail and location) for the individual, or department, responsible for this service.

- **Service hours and service availability:** Example: 'Between 9 am and 6 pm, with an availability of 95% to 97% uptime.'

- **User and customer support:** Example: 'All users can call extension 777 during office hours, for any support issue.'

- **Charges:** Example: 'A monthly fee of £25 will be charged to the business unit or project for this service.'

- **Other relevant details**.

Some tips and advice for a service catalogue

- A service catalogue cannot be complete or final from day one. It should be completed in small steps. The initial catalogue should be planned internally within IT, with representation from all stakeholders. The team should create a list of all IT services the organisation owns, and then start including them one by one in a catalogue after considering the pros, cons, support issues, costs and risks of providing such a service to end-users. In its simplest form, a service catalogue can be a matrix, table or spreadsheet. Or you can integrate it with your CMS.

- It's a good idea to have a service catalogue for each IT department, as well as for the entire organisation.

- Each IT department should be able to answer the following questions:

  - What services do we provide?

  - What services do we *not* provide?

  - Why, why not, how, etc.

- Ask, and find out, what customers want. Find out what IT facilities other companies provide to their end-users to improve productivity, efficiency, revenue enhancement and cost saving.

- Make it simple for everyone to understand what they can get and what they cannot. Ensure that the service catalogue is written in terms that are meaningful to customers. Don't use any confusing jargon or highly technical words. Answer the questions they normally ask such as, 'I want a new computer, how do I get it?'

- Pay attention to the presentation of the information. Whether the service catalogue is a physical document or resides at a website, make sure the information is user-friendly, clear and easy to understand.

- Don't mention services that you cannot fully support or may provide at some stage in the future. Mention only guaranteed services that you can maintain properly and that are available now.

CHAPTER 12: CAPACITY MANAGEMENT

'The world would be happier if men had the same capacity to be silent that they have to speak.'

Baruch Spinoza

What is capacity management?

A general dictionary defines 'capacity' in two ways: the maximum or optimum amount that can be produced; or the ability to hold. In ITIL, capacity management is part of the service design phase of the core lifecycle that handles IT capacity for current and future business requirements. It ensures that the required capacity exists in the IT infrastructure to handle growing business demands. The IT capacity team will determine the amount of disk space and processing power required if the company has to buy a new file server for storing huge engineering drawing files. Or it may recommend the optimum bandwidth to be purchased if everyone in the organisation is to be provided with Internet access.

The ITIL definition of capacity is:

'The maximum throughput that a configuration item or IT service can deliver whilst meeting agreed service level targets. For some types of CI, capacity may be the size or volume, for example a disk drive.'

And the ITIL definition of capacity management is:

'The process responsible for ensuring that the capacity of IT services and the IT infrastructure is able to deliver agreed service level targets in a cost-effective and timely manner. Capacity management considers all resources required to deliver an IT service, and is concerned with meeting both the current and future capacity and performance needs of the business.'

Why is capacity management necessary?

Every business unit will have its own urgent demands on the IT environment, often caused by poor planning or competitive demands. New bandwidth-hungry applications may need to be installed urgently, which require sudden and massive increases in bandwidth. Failure to address these requirements will lead to an imbalance between the organisation's IT capacity and the business requirements. However, irrespective of the pressure applied, not all demands can be met immediately, as there will be several costs and other dependencies. Only some can be met immediately, others will have to wait, and some cannot be met at all for numerous reasons. If large amounts of disk space are required for storing important data and the servers in the organisation are small-disk models, then end-users will not be able to store their data securely. There could also be several such capacity-related issues that need attention. Capacity management provides accurate guidance on how to plan, justify and manage the appropriate levels of resources needed for a given solution. Improper planning for capacity can lead to wasted resources, unnecessary expenses, poor performance or frequent disruption to business.

Some of the key benefits of having capacity management are:

- Ensuring proper IT capacity for current, future and sudden demands (*see example overleaf*).

- Avoiding incorrect capacity which could result in costly issues later on.

- Better and optimal use of IT equipment.

- Knowing when and where to spend.

- Preventing frequent upgrades, equipment downtime and associated costs.

- Constantly coordinate with demand management and other departments to ensure adequate IT capacity at all times.

Example: Inadequate capacity

Manager: 'Hello, help desk. We are getting seven new design engineers tomorrow. Can you provide computers and e-mail IDs to them immediately? Also, they will all need that design software installed in each of the computers.'

Help desk: 'Sorry. Not possible. We don't have any spare computers. Also, we don't have any additional design software licenses or free disk space on your engineering server.'

Manager: 'But those engineers will need to start work on a project for an important client from tomorrow. How long will it take to get new computers and other stuff?'

Help desk: 'No idea, maybe four weeks.'

Manager: '*Four weeks!*'

Figure 13 illustrates the differences between inadequate and adequate capacity management.

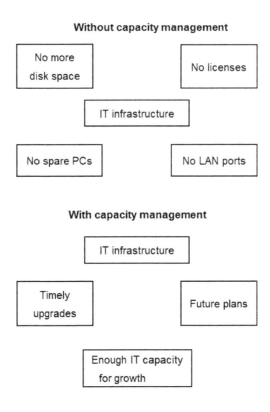

Figure 13: Inadequate and adequate capacity management

What are the responsibilities of capacity management?

One of the key responsibilities of capacity management is to understand current and future business requirements, and to try and fulfil them in a cost-effective manner. The principal responsibilities of capacity management are:

- Business capacity management
- Service capacity management

- Resource capacity management.

A fuller explanation of each is as follows:

- **Business capacity management:** Here the capacity management team is responsible for ensuring that the future business requirements for IT services are studied, planned and implemented in a cost-effective and timely fashion. Requirements for the future usually come from the various business managers, business plans and forecasts. For example, a RockSolid Corp business plan may propose increasing employee strength from the existing 1,000 employees to about 1,500 within a year. Capacity management will have to study the growth plan and propose necessary increases in the number of computers, disk space, software licenses, bandwidth and telephones, required by all those new employees. Additionally, the new equipment will have to be procured, installed and made ready well before the new employees join.

- **Service capacity management:** This area focuses on the performance of current services used by the business. It studies the current IT services, how they are being used and peak usages, and ensures that the services can meet their SLA targets. It tries to ensure that committed performance of the various services meets the business requirements. If hundreds of new computers are purchased and installed, the service capacity team must also ensure that the incident management team and service desk is capable of supporting all those new machines, and ensure committed turnaround times for support calls.

- **Resource capacity management:** Here, the capacity management team is concerned with identifying and understanding the capacity and utilisation of various CIs in the organisation. This process can study whether all file servers are being used optimally, or whether some servers are overloaded or underutilised. It can then make necessary recommendations to ensure even utilisation.

What are the tools used by capacity management?

Capacity management relies on collecting data from various sources, including discussions with concerned staff, incident management and problem management. Some of the methods used are:

- **Monitoring tools:** Nowadays, several monitoring tools are available that can monitor activities on various types of IT equipment, e.g. servers, routers, bandwidth, etc. These tools can generate reports and logs of how they are being utilised. For example, a bandwidth-monitoring tool on a network can give reports on how much bandwidth is being used on a particular line during peak and lean periods.

- **Modelling tools:** These tools can be used for conducting load simulation. For example, a modelling tool can predict how a piece of software or hardware can deteriorate in performance when the load hits a maximum.

- **Reporting tools and reports:** These are tools that can generate reports on how the existing equipment is being used. For example, a disk space monitoring tool can give a report on how much data is being pumped into a hard disk per day and per week. Based on the trend, capacity management can recommend an increase in disk capacity to handle future requirements.

There are other inputs from staff, and other experience-based decisions, that can assist in proper capacity planning. For example, experience can suggest that it is necessary for every end-user to have a minimum of 20 gigabytes of disk space on the local hard disks, considering the number of applications to be installed.

What is meant by a capacity database?

A capacity database (also known as a capacity management database) is a database used by all activities in capacity management and which contains technical, business, financial, service and utilisation data. It contains all relevant data required by the capacity management team to produce management information to take appropriate decisions to increase or decrease capacity. For example, if the capacity management team has observed that only 20 of the 50 file servers are being actively used, it may recommend a reduction in the remaining 30 servers. On the other hand, if it notices that 50 servers are not enough to handle existing and future amounts of data, it may recommend an upgrade of disk capacities, or the purchase of additional servers.

What is meant by an IT staff ratio?

Most organisations only concentrate on having enough disk space, bandwidth, laptops and processing power, and conveniently forget, or ignore, the human side of capacity management. In order to maintain a large IT infrastructure, it is also necessary to have a sufficient number of IT staff, in the respective areas, to properly manage the various systems. Irrespective of the amount of automation and automatic systems, enough qualified staff are still needed to understand, control, manage and run the operations. The dangers of having a bad ratio are obvious. It is similar to teacher-child ratios in schools, or nurse-patient ratios in hospitals. However, many organisations fail to understand this important aspect, and try to keep the absolute minimum number of IT staff, or a very small team, to maintain a large IT infrastructure. The standard decision factors are cost saving and businesses unable, or unwilling, to invest in more headcount.

Many business and even IT managers think that it is a waste of money to have more IT staff. However, managing a large IT infrastructure will put enormous pressure on the entire staff if the IT department is too small. Naturally, this will result in frequent resignations, improper process compliance, delay in support, heated arguments and other issues that will slowly engulf the organisation. In fact, it is a big risk to an organisation to have inadequate IT staff. Sudden resignations and accidents can strangle an organisation. Imagine what would happen if RockSolid Corp had just one experienced administrator to manage the company website, or a critical customised database, and he or she suddenly met with an accident. A newcomer, or a vendor, would not be able to suddenly take over, understand and start managing the organisation's website or database.

It is not enough for organisations to say they have implemented ITIL by simply preparing a series of process documents, procedures and policies, but not to have the correct number of staff to practice ITIL in the recommended way. Additionally, there is no point in committing high levels of availability everywhere, when there is a shortage of staff to provide even the basic services. This is where staff ratio will help. Most IT departments worldwide are struggling to meet service expectations that are too high for the current sizes of their IT departments. An IT staff ratio means having the correct number of IT staff for a certain number of end-users and IT equipment. A general rule of thumb is to have two IT staff members to support about 100 end-users, using 100 computers, and about three or four servers. However, it would be unreasonable to have the same two IT staff members continue to support the organisation when the strength grows to 200 end-users. The IT staff will have to increase in direct proportion to the end-users count. Many business managers may argue that it is possible to simply implement a few fancy tools and not increase IT staff. However, such arguments usually do not work out in the real world. Fancy tools are usually very expensive, and will anyway need highly qualified staff to operate and maintain, plus there will be substantial ongoing costs. So it is absolutely necessary for businesses to ensure that they have the correct IT staff strength to maintain the expected levels of availability. However, there is no magic number for an IT staff ratio.

Organisations will have to gather the following statistics and arrive at an optimum number:

- Average number of end-user calls per day

- Average number of call backlogs per day

- Call response time compared to committed time

- User downtime

- User downtime calculated in financial terms

- Growth of end-user count.

A company that wishes to compete based on properly fulfilling commitments made to external customers must invest in the correct IT staff-end-user ratios, to remain competitive. Otherwise, the company could slowly suffer from internal decay that could soon paralyse the business. The revenue loss due to an overloaded, understaffed IT service team providing poor service, will be several times the savings in salaries of *not* having twice the number of IT staff. Sometimes even a couple of hours delay in IT support could affect the business:

Example: Inadequate staff ratio affecting business

A computer could fail during an important business presentation to a potential client. As you may have observed, computers always fail at the most inappropriate time. If there were enough IT staff, a techie could speedily attend the issue within minutes to give an immediate workaround, thereby giving a good impression to the client about the organisation's service standards. Conversely, if there were a shortage of staff and the techie drops in after two hours, it could lead to a rise in tempers, acute embarrassment, an abrupt end to the meeting, or even the loss of the client (a very high probability).

Some tips and advice for capacity management

- When buying any IT equipment or software licenses, ensure you do not buy the specifications or quantities that will exactly meet the current requirements. IT is an exponential beast. If you buy a computer with just 4 gigabytes hard disk, to save some costs initially, over a system with an 8 gigabyte disk, it may suit your present need. However, if the system needs to load another application or a critical upgrade, such as an anti-virus program or an operating system upgrade, a couple of months later, you may discover the hard disk is not sufficient to sustain the upgrade. So always buy equipment that will easily suit planned or unplanned upgrades for at least a couple of years, wherever possible. Similarly, buy enough numbers of common and necessary software to ensure you don't need to run and buy another license when the next request arrives.

- Check utilisation of servers, disk space and bandwidth at regular intervals. Set thresholds for each. Increase capacity or optimise usage when they start crossing the thresholds.

- Ensure that the asset management teams have enough spares of critical equipment, such as computers, laptops, printers, hard disks, software licenses and memory that can be deployed speedily when the need arises.

- Think big when it comes to servers, data centres and bandwidth. The usage and utilisation of equipment, or services, can grow very rapidly within months, or even weeks. If you design a small data centre suiting your current need, you may soon face a situation where you have no space to add ten more servers. Data centres simply cannot be expanded without heaps of work, associated costs and downtime.

- The capacity management team will periodically need to meet with practically all IT departments and business managers to understand their current and future needs, and to decide what must be purchased, or upgraded, over the next few months.

- Capacity management, in liaison with demand management, must also recommend consolidation and/or distribution of equipment around the organisation, as required to optimise usage of assets. For example, there could be a common printer that is suffering from overload, while there could be two printers in the marketing department that are hardly used.

What are the sub-processes of capacity management?

Capacity management has the following sub-processes.

Business capacity management: This involves translating business needs and plans into capacity and performance requirements for services and IT infrastructure. It also ensures that future capacity and performance needs can be fulfilled.

Service capacity management: This process manages, controls and predicts the performance and capacity of operational services. This includes initiating proactive and reactive action to ensure that the performances and capacities of services meet their agreed targets.

Component capacity management: This process manages, controls and predicts the performance, utilisation and capacity of IT resources and individual IT components.

Capacity management reporting: This process provides other service management processes and IT management with information related to service and resource capacity, utilisation and performance.

CHAPTER 13: DEMAND MANAGEMENT

'Teach a parrot the terms "supply and demand" and you've got an economist.'

Thomas Carlyle

What is demand?

A general dictionary defines demand in several ways. The one that applies to IT is any urgent or pressing requirement for one or more specific IT services. The requirement can be for a new service, or an upgrade to an existing service that is currently performing inadequately.

What is demand management?

Demand management is a sub-process of service strategy. Demand management is still closely interconnected with capacity management, but can be viewed as one step higher and being more strategic in nature, as it can influence sharing and redistributing an organisation's resources optimally.

Whether it is an increase in employees, downsizing, mergers, takeovers and outsourcing, the IT department will have sudden increases in work. Often, due to business growth or competition, it becomes necessary to make massive increases in IT capacity within a short period of time. In IT, everything is urgent and must happen right now. Business managers expect IT to provide fast, innovative solutions to chaotic business changes.

13: Demand Management

Demand can be in two ways:

1. There could be a demand for new IT services. For example, demands for technical support for a latest operating system for a set of end-users.

2. There could be usage demand on already existing IT services that end-users and the business feel is currently inadequate. For example, a need for Internet line usage and disk space usage beyond what is currently available. If 50 new users are added to the network and start using the same existing Internet lease line, it may get overloaded and require some tuning or a speedy increase in bandwidth, at additional cost.

Not all of these demands can be executed in a leisurely way. If an organisation hires 50 new employees or contractors for a new project, this can become an instant workload increase for the IT department to supply and install computers, e-mail IDs and the necessary software. In addition, there will be background activities, such as enabling network ports, server disk space allocation and security management. All these activities can be classified as a 'demand' on IT services. All such demands need proper control and management. This is where a professional demand management process can help.

As mentioned before, there can be several unpredictable and urgent requirements by business managers on IT services. Very often it is not possible to say 'no', or delay the fulfilment, as there will be several competitive and internal compulsions. So what usually happens is the techies will be put under a lot of pressure, with unrealistic workloads to meet those requirements. Also, such an upsurge in the workload can put a severe strain on several other departments and external vendors, to meet the demand. This can result in interdepartmental conflicts and other issues.

Demand management prevents such issues from happening, by taking proactive steps to increase capacity or meet sudden demands.

The ITIL definition of demand management is:

'The process responsible for understanding, anticipating and influencing customer demand for services. Demand management works with capacity management to ensure that the service provider has sufficient capacity to meet the required demand. At a strategic level, demand management can involve analysis of patterns of business activity and user profiles, while at a tactical level, it can involve the use of differential charging to encourage customers to use IT services at less busy times, or require short-term activities to respond to unexpected demand or the failure of a configuration item.'

What are the responsibilities of demand management?

Some of the main responsibilities of demand management are as follows:

- Demand management optimises and rationalises the use of existing IT resources.

- Demand management is responsible for redistributing capacity in order to ensure that critical services are not affected, or at least to minimise the impact on them.

- Demand management reviews capacity requirements from both a long-term and short-term perspective.

- Demand management should be capable of handling planned and unplanned demands. Planned demand can be part of the annual, or half-yearly, IT planning process, which outlines what has to purchased or implemented. Unplanned demand may be a rush of huge amounts of unpredictable work.

Some tips and advice for demand management

Having a demand management department can be of immense value to an organisation, to save costs and rationalise usage of IT equipment and resources.

- **Do not fulfil unnecessary or unrealistic demands:** Having a demand management process does not mean every demand or threat by the end-users, or business, will be immediately met. It is not a wish-fulfilment department, and does not meet unnecessary or unrealistic demands. If the existing computers have sufficient processing power and capacity to run all the available applications, then you must not accept a demand to buy new high-powered models just because end-users fancy having a new one.

- **Redistribute equipment to where it is needed most and best utilised:** Demand management should concentrate efforts on areas that are suffering from capacity issues. In most organisations, the IT capacity and equipment will be unevenly used. There will be excess IT capacity in some departments, while there will be famine in others. Often departments that have no need for high computing power or heavy-duty equipment will, nevertheless, have such equipment for political reasons, budget powers and other issues. Elsewhere, departments that really need such equipment and power may be suffering from low-powered systems and inadequate resources. Demand management can look into such issues and redistribute equipment. It may not be easy, but it should not be impossible if properly approved organisational processes and policies are put in place. For example, there could be three lightly used printers in a department, while another department that has heavy printing needs may have only one printer. Demand management can intervene here and reallocate the printers to the department that really needs them.

- **Check before upgrading:** It is not recommended that you blindly increase capacity if end-users face issues. The issues could be due to an improperly configured server, or networking equipment that needs to be tackled first. Similarly, assess whether the workload can be redistributed without increasing capacity.

- **Support from management:** Demand management can be effective only if all the IT equipment and services in an organisation are owned by the IT department, and not by individual departments. Also, senior management have to support optimisation and rationalisation. Experienced IT managers know that a lot of equipment and services are either underutilised or overused in their organisation. However, they will not be in a position to rearrange and redistribute equipment, due to political reasons and department clashes. For example, a senior manager may have a heavy-duty laser printer for his department but not allow other departments to take printouts. In such cases, professional demand management can step in and make it a shared printer for everyone to use.

- **Being prepared for sudden demands:** Demand management must always be prepared to handle sudden surges in IT demands, due to pressing business requirements. Often there will be abrupt IT demands, very common in many projects due to poor planning or irrational customer demands. Or there could be some sudden mergers, acquisitions, takeovers and reorganisations that can suddenly place a huge workload on IT. For example, if there is a sudden need to add a few hundred computers to the network, demand management must be able to step in with capacity and supplier management to locate a suitable vendor capable of implementing and configuring hundreds of computers within a short time.

CHAPTER 14: AVAILABILITY MANAGEMENT

'Work expands so as to fill the time available for its completion. General recognition of this fact is shown in the proverbial phrase "It is the busiest man who has time to spare".'

C Northcote Parkinson

What is availability?

A general dictionary defines availability as something that is ready for use or accessible when required. In ITIL, availability refers to the accessibility of the various infrastructure and services provided by IT services during the stated time periods.

The ITIL definition of availability is:

'Ability of an IT service or other configuration item to perform its agreed function when required. Availability is determined by reliability, maintainability, serviceability, performance and security. Availability is usually calculated as a percentage. This calculation is often based on agreed service time and downtime. It is best practice to calculate availability of an IT service using measurements of the business output.'

What is availability management?

Availability management is part of the service design phase of the ITSM core lifecycle. Availability management is the necessary precaution, prevention and activities that need to be carried out by IT services to ensure that the various committed IT services are available to end-users during the committed time periods. The IT department may commit to all end-users that the availability of the company e-mail servers is *assured* between 8 am and 8 pm on all days, except for any emergencies. Equally, they may commit an availability of 95% in a month, calculated on a 24/7 basis. Availability management involves anticipating and preventing failures, maintenance activities, ensuring security, monitoring and recoverability. Unless there are unanticipated issues, such assurances must be upheld by the IT department.

The ITIL definition of availability management is:

'The process responsible for ensuring that IT services meet the current and future availability needs of the business in a cost-effective and timely manner. Availability management defines, analyses, plans, measures and improves all aspects of the availability of IT services, and ensures that all IT infrastructures, processes, tools, roles etc. are appropriate for the agreed service level targets for availability.'

Why is availability management important?

Customers and businesses depend on IT for most of their needs. An organisation's mission-critical systems must be online and accessible at all times because there will be many subsystems, departments and even external customers that will be connected and dependent on them. High availability is very important to most organisations. End-users must be able to send and receive e-mails whenever they want, during office hours, so IT services must take the necessary precautions and maintenance activities to ensure that the e-mail servers are online during office hours. This means that they should not install upgrades, or releases, or do restarts on the systems (except for emergencies), during the stated period.

Example: Poor availability management

End-user: 'Hello, help desk. I am not able to access my e-mail. What is wrong with the server?'

Help desk: 'Nothing is wrong. We just shut it down to upgrade some memory and do other maintenance on the server.'

End-user: 'But it is Monday morning. We need the server to send some important e-mails. When will it be online?'

Help desk: 'Probably by late evening or tomorrow.'

End-user: '*Tomorrow*? But you can't shut down systems during working hours without advance notice. You folks should inform us in advance before you shut down.'

Help desk: 'Okay, maybe next time.'

Experienced IT professionals will tell you that people or process failures cause the biggest proportion of equipment downtime. The remaining portion is usually caused by technology failures and power failures. IT systems and applications are extremely complex and must be managed with proper operational disciplines. The complexity of IT infrastructures and applications makes management of 'high-availability' systems very difficult. Every precaution must be taken before anybody is allowed to meddle with any mission-critical, or important, system or application. As mentioned earlier, most CIs have relationships with several other CIs. An unexpected change in one can cause undesirable changes in the others, and may even result in extended downtime and disrupt the business.

Figure 14 illustrates the differences between having no availability management and having an adequate system in place.

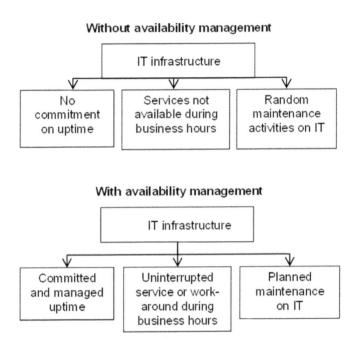

Figure 14: Inadequate and adequate availability management

What are the main responsibilities of availability management?

Some of the key responsibilities are:

- Determining availability requirements from the business
- Determining vital business functions
- Business impact analysis

- Defining targets for availability
- Monitoring and trend analysis
- Reporting.

A fuller explanation of each is as follows:

Determining availability: Availability is one of the key SLA elements often requested by business operations. This will involve discussions with business managers and end-users to determine the optimum availability expected for all important equipment. The business and end-users may specify that they will need access to their e-mail and file servers between 8 am and 4 pm every business day. Or a certain project may demand that they have access to their project file servers in the night, between 9 pm and 3 am, to suit a specific time zone. So the availability management teams, and the service level management teams, must put their heads together and ensure that the required business demands are met, or workarounds provided.

Determining vital business functions: Here, the availability management team must study and document which of the several IT systems is critical for the business. For example, of the dozens of servers in the organisation, only a few may be really critical to the business. So availability management must liaise with service continuity management (covered in *Chapter 17*), to ensure those critical systems have the necessary availability and also have adequate disaster recovery facilities.

Business impact analysis: Here, availability management may calculate the loss or impact in terms of revenue or business risk if a particular service is not available for end-users. Assume that the organisation had ten external consultants who were paid £100 an hour each. All the consultants work on an application installed on a particular server. If that particular server was down for three hours during the time those consultants work, then the organisation will suffer a loss of £3,000 that will still be paid to those consultants without any productive work. In another example, if the company's purchase order system is down, causing several purchase orders to be delayed beyond committed delivery dates, the company may run the risk of losing those orders to their competitor and also suffer a loss of reputation due to not fulfilling orders on time.

Defining targets for availability: After studying the various business requirements, availability management may recommend a committed availability target for various systems.

Table 18 gives an example reference source for the availability of IT services to end-users.

Table 18: The availability of IT services to end-users

System or service	Total hours per month	Agreed or promised availability (%)	Agreed or promised availability (hours)	Downtime tolerated	Window
Purchase order system	264	98%	259	5	8 am-8 pm
E-mail systems	264	95%	251	13	8 am-8 pm
Engineering servers	264	90%	238	26	8 am-5 pm

Total hours calculation: 264 hours = 22 business days per month @ 12 hours per day. Saturday and Sunday are holidays.

Actual availability: 264 minus number of hours downtime per month.

Availability: % = [Actual availability/Agreed availability] x 100

An availability calculation for the purchase order system every month, whose committed availability is 98%, would be as follows:

March: If there were no issues between 8 am and 8 pm on all days then the system was actually available for a full 264 hours. This means the system was available without trouble for greater than 98% or 259 hours of agreed or promised availability. This means in March the availability percentage exceeded the commitment percentage as calculated by [(264/259) x 100] = 101.9%.

April: If there were issues and the system was actually available for exactly 259 hours, then the availability was exactly 98% or 259 hours (as promised). This means in April the availability percentage met the commitment percentage exactly as calculated by [(259/259) x 100] = 100%.

May: If there were more issues, and the system was actually available only for 240 hours, then the availability was close to about 92.6% (less than committed): [(240/259) x 100] using the same calculations as above.

Monitoring and trend analysis: It is also possible to study measurements, such as mean time between failures (MTBF) and mean time to repair (MTTR), to get a picture of the availability. An MTBF will tell you the average time between restoration of a service due to an incident and another incident occurring. An MTTR will tell you the average downtime between an incident occurring and the restoration of the service or system.

Reports: All of these can be generated as individual or consolidated reports for management. Based on the reports and trends, suitable action can be taken to ensure optimum availability, by installing rugged systems or having proper maintenance and spares.

Some tips and advice for availability management

- Do not plan any routine maintenance activities, minor or major, during office hours. Plan all maintenance activities after office hours in the event of any unforeseen issues arising. A techie may feel a small service pack upgrade on a server is a minor issue, but if the patch had a bug, it could bring down the server during office hours and lead to chaos in the organisation.

- Ensure an adequate supply of critical spares within the organisation. This way, if a part fails, the techies can speedily replace the failed unit and prevent downtime caused by the delay of a vendor getting the required spare from his office.

- Ensure that the IT operations management teams carry out necessary and periodic maintenance on all critical equipment, to prevent downtime and shutdowns due to improper or insufficient maintenance.

What are the sub-processes of availability management?

Availability management has the following sub-processes.

Design services for availability: This process will design the procedures and technical features required to fulfil the agreed availability levels.

Availability testing: This process will make sure that all availability, resilience and recovery mechanisms are subject to regular testing.

Availability monitoring and reporting: This process will provide other service management processes and IT management with information related to service and component availability. This includes comparing achieved vs. agreed availability and the identification of areas where availability must be improved.

CHAPTER 15: INFORMATION SECURITY MANAGEMENT

'The only thing that makes life possible is permanent, intolerable uncertainty; not knowing what comes next.'

Ursula K LeGuin

What is information security?

Organisations rely on several types of data for their business, and can suffer from various disasters if critical information and data are compromised by any means. Some of the information contained in them can be confidential and must not be viewed, or altered, by unauthorised persons. The salary details of all your employees cannot be made public for everyone to know or view. This could lead to your company payment website being breached and defaced by hackers, causing a loss of reputation and other disasters. It is necessary to have a protective envelope around the various kinds of data that an organisation uses, to prevent unauthorised people from accessing it. This is information security (IS), and has to be managed by a security team on a continuous basis. Information security management is part of the service design phase of the ITSM core lifecycle. Information security is a vast subject by itself and only very brief details are provided here. The following portal has substantial information on security data and resources:

IT Governance: *www.itgovernance.co.uk/infosec.aspx*.

The ITIL definition of information security management is:

'The process that ensures the confidentiality, integrity and availability of an organisation's assets, information, data and IT services. Information security management usually forms part of an organisational approach to security management which has a wider scope than the IT service provider, and includes handling of paper, building access, phone calls, etc. for the entire organisation.'

What are the various ways in which information security can be compromised?

As mentioned earlier, disasters can happen to organisations if information security is compromised in any one of a number of different ways:

- An organisation connected to the Internet can be hacked by unauthorised persons if there is no proper firewall, intrusion detection or anti-virus system. A firewall will prevent an organisation's internal IP network being visible to the outside world. An intrusion detection system will spot suspicious activities happening on the network. An intrusion detection system can detect if some rogue software program is initiating a denial of service (DoS) attack on a website.

- A laptop containing confidential and sensitive information can be stolen.

- Confidential documents can be scanned, or photocopied, by unauthorised staff.

- Unauthorised personnel can intercept sensitive e-mails.

- Unauthorised persons may get access to data centres.

- Tapes, CD-ROMS and other removable media containing confidential data can fall into the wrong hands.

- External consultants, contractors and vendors working within an organisation can view, or access, confidential data they are not supposed to see.

- Carelessness and human error in allowing unauthorised persons to get passwords, entry by strangers, etc.

- Critical passwords getting lost, stolen or changed by unauthorised persons.

- Somebody can hack a company website and alter, or steal, sensitive information. If an organisation sells products over the Internet, somebody can hack into the website and collect customer information, such as credit card numbers and e-mail IDs.

- Employees who resign, or get fired, may destroy important data before they leave, or pass on sensitive information to outsiders.

What safeguards are available to protect information?

To prevent information from being compromised, an organisation should first classify all its data appropriately, and ensure proper safeguards for each. Some common examples of classifying company data are:

- **Confidential:** Only the employee, and certain types of employees, such as HR and finance, should know an employee's salary: it should not be visible for others.

- **Secure or restricted:** Only authorised staff should handle the passwords of mission-critical systems and production servers.

- **Internal or private:** General company policies can be made visible to all employees via the company intranet.

- **Levels of importance:** A software development team can classify its software code as important and restrict access to certain team members only.

- **General or public:** Certain information, such as fire safety, health tips and first aid, can be classified as general and displayed for everyone.

Other safeguards can be of several different types, depending on the nature of an organisation. Some of the common precautions you can take are as follows:

- All confidential data can be housed in a secure file server with access only by the authorised department's personnel. The administrative password can be kept in a secure safe and all usage logged in a register.

- All important data can be stored in secure file servers that can be accessed only by authorised employees.

- People can be prevented from printing, photocopying or e-mailing certain types of documents. For example, it is possible to convert many types of document into an Adobe® pdf file but then have printing disabled to make it read-only.

- Ensuring that all hard copies of confidential documents are shredded after use, so that they do not fall into the hands of unauthorised persons.

- Ensuring that nobody stores important data on laptops, CD-ROMS and other removable media that can easily get misplaced or stolen.

- Electronic systems can be implemented to log and monitor activities on all computers, or only those of certain users.

- Preventing and monitoring Internet access of every employee. Ensure they do not access chat sites and non-business sites.

- Prevent Internet and external e-mail access to certain highly sensitive profiles if possible. This is to prevent unscrupulous employees sending details, such as the credit card information and account information of customers to online criminals.

- Prevent users from bringing video phones, mobile cameras and fancy communication gadgets into the organisation.

- Information security is a very wide topic and encompasses several areas. It is recommended this be the responsibility of a separate department in your organisation.

Example: A military organisation protecting its data

One of the companies that the author was working for in the Middle East had supplied several computers to a large defence organisation. Security and movement of materials were extremely tight. The author's company was maintaining the hardware. However, whenever there was a hardware fault, like a hard disk failure, there would be two qualified defence personnel meticulously supervising the disk replacement by the IT vendor. Even after replacing the failed hard disk with a new one, they would not allow the vendor to take the failed hard disk back, irrespective of the nature of the fault, for security reasons.

Some tips and advice for information security management

- Information security is a vast subject by itself, and there are plenty of consultants, white papers and best practices that can teach you how to implement information security. Organisations must take assistance from such sources, to implement a sound information security department in their organisation.

- It is not enough if all relevant policies are prepared and just published. They must be put into practice by all employees, in an orderly manner. Information security must be continuously enforced with the help of an access management department (explained in *Chapter 16*).

- Have a series of information security policies for your organisation. Such policies can be purchased from various sources and customised to your organisation's needs.

- Indulge in exhaustive and periodic user education on information security through seminars, videos, contests, quizzes, posters and reward programmes.

- Install a state of the art firewall (hardware or software) between the company network and the Internet. Firewalls prevent a hacker sitting on the Internet from snooping into an organisation's network. Excellent firewalls are available from many companies.

- Install all manufacturer-recommended patches, hot fixes and service packs, on all computers. These patches fix various vulnerabilities that can be exploited to hack into a machine.

- Log all accesses into and out of your network using special tools that can detect which computer accessed your systems. Using the latest logging tools you can identify exactly the IP address and other details of the computer that accessed your credit card system. It is even possible to pinpoint whether it's located in some other country.

- Change critical passwords often and ensure that they are not easy to guess, for example, 'blank', 'password' and 'secret'. Have a combination of alpha-numeric and uppercase/lowercase letters.

- Always have the latest anti-virus update on all critical systems.

- As an added precaution, purchase, and install, personal firewalls on computers. This software can detect and alert a user if some other computer is trying to access his or her computer. Personal firewall software helps prevent people from hacking into your computer while you are on the Internet. A personal firewall can help make your computer impenetrable to hackers. However, as with anti-virus programs, it is important that you keep your personal firewall software up to date.

- Install spyware and adware removers. Spyware and adware are tiny programs that install themselves, without your permission, while you are browsing the web. Anti-virus programs cannot usually detect such programs. Depending on how it is written, these tiny programs can send out sensitive information without the user's knowledge.

- Do not open suspicious e-mail attachments. The attachments can contain a Trojan virus or a program designed to wreak havoc on your computer. A Trojan is a computer program which, when running, allows a hacker to gain easy access to your computer system. Users cannot see that a Trojan program is running on their computer. Some Trojans allow hackers to take control of your computer system.

- Don't download stuff recklessly from the Internet. Websites designed by troublemakers provide software which is intentionally designed to hack and damage your computer.

What are the sub-processes of information security?

Information security has the following sub-processes.

Design of security controls: This process designs appropriate technical and organisational measures to ensure the confidentiality, integrity, security and availability of an organisation's assets, information, data and services.

Security testing: This process makes sure that all security mechanisms are subject to regular testing.

Management of security incidents: This process detects and fights attacks and intrusions, and minimises the damage incurred by security breaches.

Security review: This process reviews if security measures and procedures are still in line with risk perceptions from the business side, and verifies if those measures and procedures are regularly maintained and tested.

CHAPTER 16: ACCESS MANAGEMENT

'It is what we prevent, rather than what we do that counts most in Government.'

W L Mackenzie King

What is access management?

Access management aims to grant authorised users the right to use a service, while preventing access to non-authorised users. An organisation can have several computers, network equipment, servers and databases required for its business. Naturally, all equipment cannot, and should not, be accessible to every user or department. The important designs stored in a folder on an engineering server should be accessible only to the engineering staff, and not to every employee in the office. So, IT departments must ensure access is provided only to authorised persons, and prevent unauthorised persons from viewing or modifying them. An access management department's job is to enforce all the previously designed and published information security policies of an organisation. Access management teams do not define security standards, though their inputs may be considered for upgrading or modifying a policy. Access management separates operational and execution activities from strategic and design ones. Access management is part of the service operation phase of the core lifecycle. Access management is sometimes also referred to as rights management or identity management.

The ITIL definition of access management is:

'The process responsible for allowing users to make use of IT services, data, or other assets. Access management helps to protect the confidentiality, integrity and availability of assets by ensuring that only authorised users are able to access or modify the assets. Access management is sometimes referred to as rights management or identity management.'

What are the responsibilities of access management?

The main responsibilities are:

1. Handling access requests

2. Verification

3. Providing rights

4. Monitoring identity status

5. Logging and tracking access

6. Removing or restricting access.

A fuller explanation of each is as follows:

Requesting access: Requests for access to a system, database, server and folder can come from various areas and departments. A new design employee may want access to the engineering server that stores all designs. Or an operator may want temporary access into a data centre. Such requests may be routed via the service desk, or include the procedure for requesting access in the service catalogue. Access management will then have to act upon the request.

Verification: In a large organisation requests may come from several areas. The access management team will have to first verify and study a request, to ensure that the request is a legitimate one. If a finance assistant requests access into an engineering design server, the request management should first verify why such access should be provided to a system that is not finance related. The request may be rejected, or further details requested. Conversely, legitimate end-users must provide additional details to fully verify the request for access, in order to prevent any fraud or misrepresentation. There are many methods for verifying the end-user's identity, for example, by asking security questions, such as date of birth, employee number, social security number, signatures from an approving authority and biometric devices. Depending on the organisation, the security policies may define different levels of verification to access different services. A request to access the credit card details of customers in a banking system will need a higher level, or several levels of verification, than a request to reset a LAN password. All such procedures ensure that only authorised persons have access to critical or sensitive equipment and data.

Providing rights: Once the end-user has been correctly verified, access management has to provide the appropriate rights. They must also see if the end-user has any conflicting access, and take steps to resolve such issues based on policies. A security policy defines the right a particular individual should have and access management must grant access based on this policy.

Monitoring identity status: Over the course of time, there may be several changes that happen inside an organisation, such as reorganisations, new roles and closure of projects. Access management will have to closely monitor such changes, to revoke accesses that are no longer necessary. An end-user who has requested admin access to a critical server may move to a different project that does not require access to this server, but then fails to inform access management of the change and to remove the old rights. He or she could still have rights on the server which may lead to troubles later on.

There is no easy way to monitor when an end-user changes roles or to identity status. Access management will have to periodically conduct an organisation-wide investigation to remove, or revoke, all unnecessary or unauthorised access. Monitoring activities should include periodic reviews of access rights, to ensure that the rights are being properly used and are current. Typical events that can help access management include: announcements of job changes, reorganisations, promotions or demotions, transfers, resignation or death, retirement, disciplinary action and dismissals.

Logging and tracking access: The access management team must be in a position to give all necessary reports of who is using what system, why, and what level of access each end-user has. This will be necessary to ensure regulatory compliance, audits, or to allow an investigation, if necessary. If required by senior management, access management must be able to give a report quickly on the kind, and level of access, a particular end-user has on all the critical systems in the organisation.

Removing or restricting rights: In an organisation, end-users do not stay in the same jobs or roles forever, and so their access rights should be periodically evaluated. Access management must periodically remove, or revoke, rights of users based on established policies and staff movements. Standard procedures and policies help in easily identifying events requiring the removal or restriction of rights. Some examples are resignation, changed user roles and reorganisations.

Example: Access management in action

Developer: 'Hello, service desk. I need access to finance server FS-1. Can you enable it immediately?'

Service Desk: 'Hello. That server is a highly restricted server. Please contact the access management team on #555 first.'

Developer: 'Hello, access team. I need access to finance server FS-1. The service desk asked me to contact you first.'

Access Team: 'That server is a highly restricted server. Why do you need access to it? You are a software developer and not a finance person.'

Developer: 'I have been told to modify the payroll application software settings on that server. Hence, I need admin access to the box.'

Access Team: 'Okay, before we do that, we need two e-mail approvals, one from your manager and one from the finance manager, requesting that you be provided admin access to the box. Arrange those approvals first and then we will provide you access to the box for half a day.'

Developer: 'Thanks for the information. I will get back to you shortly.'

What are the sub-processes of access management?

Access management has the following sub-processes.

Processing of user access requests: This process requests to add, change, or revoke access rights, and to make sure that only authorised users are granted the right to use a service.

Maintenance of catalogue of user roles and access profiles: This involves making sure that the catalogue of user roles and access profiles is still appropriate for the services offered to customers, and to prevent unwanted accumulation of access rights.

CHAPTER 17: IT SERVICE CONTINUITY MANAGEMENT

'Whangdepootenawah, in the Ojibwa tongue, means disaster: an unexpected affliction that strikes hard.'

Ambrose Bierce (1842–1914)

What is service continuity management?

IT service continuity management (SCM) is part of the service design phase of the ITSM core lifecycle. Service continuity management deals with managing risks to ensure that an organisation's IT infrastructure can continue to provide some minimum services, even in the event of a scenario, such as a major IT disaster. If the entire data centre that houses all the important servers gets damaged due to a fire, electrical short circuit, or some other sudden disaster, how will your company recover? How can you ensure that it is prepared to handle such disasters? SCM prepares your organisation for speedy recovery options before, if, and when a technical disaster occurs. The ultimate choice of which disaster recovery option to choose should be made in consultation with several departments and business managers. If budgets were unlimited, it would be possible to build a twin of the entire organisation elsewhere. But such luxuries are rarely available. The SCM team must be able to provide cost-effective and acceptable disaster prevention solutions. IT service continuity management is an exhaustive subject by itself and only very brief details are provided here.

The reader can refer to several excellent books published by IT Governance Publishing on the subject of business continuity, including *Disaster Recovery and Business Continuity* by this author.

The ITIL definition of SCM is:

'The process responsible for managing risks that could seriously affect IT services. IT service continuity management ensures that the IT service provider can always provide minimum agreed service levels, by reducing the risk to an acceptable level and planning for the recovery of IT services. IT service continuity management supports business continuity management.'

Brief explanations of the terms 'disaster', 'business continuity' and 'crisis management' will now be given.

What is a disaster?

A general dictionary defines a disaster as an '*occurrence causing widespread destruction and distress, or a catastrophe*'. In a business environment, any event or crisis that adversely affects or disables your organisation's critical business functions, is a disaster. According to a number of reputable surveys and studies, hundreds of organisations worldwide go out of business every year due to disasters, many of which are fully preventable. Most small businesses cannot recover from major disasters, and even large organisations can struggle.

Disasters can come in all shapes and sizes, and from all directions. This can be explained through some examples.

Example: Fire disaster

Suppose that, due to some mishap, there was a major fire in the RockSolid Corp computer data centre, and all the main computers containing years of data and required business applications are destroyed. This would automatically mean that none of the RockSolid employees would be able to do any work. The entire business could come to a standstill within hours. Recovering from such a disaster would require a huge amount of effort, time and money. In addition, there could be losses in terms of reputation, customers, insurance and legal hassles.

Example: Technical disaster

Instead of a fire, suppose there was a serious technical fault resulting in all computers shutting down due to some deadly virus attack or a software bug. This would also mean that none of the RockSolid employees would be able to work, and business would come to a standstill. Recovering from such a disaster would also require a huge amount of effort, time and money.

Example: Lack of knowledge

Organisations can also cripple themselves due to lack of adequate knowledge, or by using penny wise and pound foolish thinking.

A small financial firm had a single computer running a financial application. The application was actually developed by a freelance programmer, for a fee. In addition, the freelancer was also maintaining the company data. Only he knew how the stuff worked and how to feed or extract data and reports for the business. Due to a power outage, the central computer disk crashed and the machine stopped booting. Fortunately (or unfortunately) it was a soft crash, meaning that the hardware was okay. Without consulting the freelance programmer, the business owner picked up the phone and called the hardware vendor who had supplied the computer. The vendor promptly sent some new techie to have a look. The techie investigated the issue and realised that the operating system had to be reloaded, and informed the business owner. The business owner simply said, *'Go ahead. Do what you want. Get our system back to working condition'*. Immediately, the techie reformatted the hard disk and reloaded the operating system. The business owner was happy that the computer got fixed without any hardware costs (computer hardware was very, very expensive in those days). Next day, the freelance programmer came to the office as usual, and all hell was let loose. The company had lost two years of data entry. This is actually a true story. The company had not invested in any back-up unit other than a few floppies, which contained outdated data anyway. You might not have guessed, but the techie was none other than the author of this book who had just started his computer career in 1989 by innocently destroying somebody's data.

What is disaster recovery?

No modern organisation can run its daily operations without computers, software, telecommunications and the Internet. Modern computer systems and networks are also extremely complex and complicated. In view of the complexity and interdependence of equipment, processes and people, disasters can strike at any point and at any time. In a highly competitive, 24/7 global business environment, the leisurely time when a business could take days and weeks to resume operations is over. If a critical computer system is not working, or is unavailable, then businesses virtually have to close down. In many cases, it is almost impossible to switch over to alternative manual or legacy processes for any length of time. Businesses must be able to resume operations quickly, almost to the exact point where they stopped when the disaster struck. Though awareness of disaster recovery is increasing everywhere, very few organisations are actually well-equipped to handle disasters and restore normal operations as swiftly as possible.

Disaster recovery (DR) is the methodical preparation and execution of all the steps that will be needed to recover from a disaster, usually one caused by technology. Disaster recovery planning is mainly *technology focused.* Technology can mean voice and data communication systems, servers and computers, databases, critical data, web servers and e-mail. Your DR plan should have tested and proven methods to tackle, and recover from, all predictable and controllable IT disasters for each of the above. If there is a critical server running crucial software, then your DR plan for that system can be a standby system in an alternative location running the identical software and having daily data synchronisation. In addition, the main system can also have disk mirroring, tape back-ups, a periodic image back-up and proper change management processes, as added precautions.

A proper DR plan is of critical importance to your business. It should be documented, and periodically updated, with key staff, contact information, locations of back-ups, recovery procedures, vendor information, contracts, communications procedures and a testing schedule. Additional elements may be necessary, depending on company size.

What is business continuity?

Business continuity (BC) ensures that certain essential business functions can continue to operate in spite of disasters striking your organisation. BC is a process that identifies various risks that threaten your organisation and provides measures to safeguard the interests of its key stakeholders, customers, reputation and brand value.

Suppose a technical or non-technical disaster strikes your organisation. Naturally, all your critical staff will be busy trying to recover from the disaster. Recovering from the disaster could range from a few minutes to several days, or never. However, it is essential in many customer-oriented organisations to ensure that certain minimum *business* functions continue to operate, even while the main disaster is being attended to. Unless the disaster is very severe and hits all areas, or is not under the control of your management, the entire organisation need not come to a standstill.

BC is mainly *business focused* and will concentrate on strategies and plans for various disaster events. BC planning will prepare business areas and organisations for surviving serious business interruptions, and provide the ability to perform certain critical business functions, even during a disruptive event. If a major disaster strikes a bank's main computer during banking hours, the bank management can speedily decide to allow customers to still deposit and withdraw a nominal amount of cash until such time as the main computer is fixed. This is business continuity, and will ensure that customers have some minimal acceptable service in spite of a disaster. Having business continuity will also help preserve the company's reputation and image.

Important note

A business continuity solution need not always be a technical one, though there could be a technical disaster. Business continuity is all about providing speedy, workable alternatives to minimise adverse impact. Anything that meets this purpose can be classified as business continuity. For example, if your entire data centre that houses all the important servers gets damaged in a fire, electrical short circuit, or some other sudden disaster, your BCM team should assist in recovering the company from such situations in previously planned ways. Your business continuity management team should prepare your organisation for disaster recovery options before, if, and when a disaster occurs.

What is crisis management?

Depending on the nature of a disaster, it may be necessary for your organisation to convene a group of senior managers to control adverse media reports, handle customer satisfaction and prevent customers deserting. This is crisis management. Crisis management is also panic prevention. In the event of a major disaster in a reputable organisation with no crisis management team, there could be a possibility of a newspaper publishing a negative report, causing adverse impacts on the business, stock price and its reputation. The media can often blow a simple issue out of proportion, causing widespread panic and mayhem. A crisis management function becomes important to protect your business from such situations. A crisis management team can ensure that such situations and possibilities are controlled, by proactively taking measures to minimise losses of various kinds, including reputation losses.

Table 19 gives examples of SCM concepts.

Table 19: Summary and examples of SCM concepts

Disaster	A reputed bank's main computer's hard disk fails on Monday morning during peak banking hours. Banking operations get halted. Customers cannot verify account balances or carry out any electronic transactions.
Disaster recovery (DR)	Technical staff repair the computer by replacing the hard disk and restoring data as fast as possible. Repair and restore could take several hours, or more than a day.
Business continuity (BC)	Bank management allows all customers to withdraw up to £1,000 manually, by filling in and signing a paper withdrawal slip. Other transactions are also done by completing paper forms. Paper information will be fed into the main computer later.
Crisis management (CM)	Senior executives of the bank assure customers that the technical trouble will not cause any financial loss or improper accounting for anyone.

Why is service continuity important?

Organisations have become extremely dependent on technology for their day-to-day operations. As mentioned before, it is not possible for any modern organisation to switch over to manual processes for any length of time. It is not possible to switch back to manual typewriters, postal services, hand-written documents and spreadsheets if the entire computer and e-mail network is down. Another important concern is that any major damage to the infrastructure can result in severe financial losses, loss of reputation and even closure of the business. Most companies are interconnected and linked to the outside world via the Internet. Any technology, or other major failures in the company, can result in the company being cut off from the rest of the world.

In summary, some of the main reasons why service continuity is important are:

- Businesses have become extremely dependent on IT, so failures in IT are more likely to affect the business, and that impact is more likely to be severe.

- IT environments have become extremely complex and interrelated, so the number of potential failure points is increasing day by day.

- When IT fails, there is not enough time to recover at a leisurely pace, due to business, end-user and customer demands.

The role of a professional SCM is essential for any organisation to ensure speedy recovery and remain in business.

Example: A disaster striking the data centre

Building Security: 'Hello, Mr CIO. This is the Building Security Officer calling. Sorry to wake you at 2 am, but there has been a fire.'

CIO: 'Oh no. What was the damage?'

Building Security: 'Not much, I think. The fire engine came within 20 minutes and doused out the fire. The fireman said it had only damaged a couple of computers. The fire didn't spread to other areas.'

CIO: 'That's a relief. Any idea which computers were damaged?'

Building Security: 'Yes. Two large, black computers in the data centre. The ones with blinking green lights that were labelled Mainframe 1 and 2. They're burnt to a crisp, along with the cassettes that were stored behind them.'

CIO: 'Mainframe 1 and 2 and our back-up tapes? *Help!*'

What are the main responsibilities of SCM?

The primary responsibility of SCM is to ensure business continuity in the event of any disaster. This is done by ensuring that the required IT services can be recovered within agreed time-frames. It may not be possible for most modern businesses to tolerate more than one day's non-availability of IT services. So IT SCM has to make all necessary arrangements to restore services within a day, should a disaster occur.

IT SCM has four main responsibilities:

1. Initiation
2. Requirements and strategy
3. Implementation
4. Ongoing operational management.

A fuller explanation of each is as follows:

Initiation: Most organisations do not have any true disaster recovery or business continuity processes in place. Often, disaster recovery or business continuity is much more than just making data back-ups of various servers and storing them elsewhere. For an organisation to be capable of handling IT and other disasters, there are many activities that need to be carried out as an organisation-wide effort. Every business unit must get involved to provide inputs about their critical systems, and also to allocate sufficient budgets, dedicated staff and additional equipment, to initiate the service continuity mechanism.

Requirements and strategy: In this stage, the SCM team will have to perform a business impact analysis (BIA) of every business function, project and department in the organisation. A BIA is a detailed analysis of the effect and risks for the business if a specific set of IT services is not available. It will also identify the minimum set of services that an organisation will need to continue operating. A detailed analysis can be carried out to find out what will be the business impact if the company's purchase order server is blown to pieces due to some disaster. How will the department function without its core system? In the event that it does happen, what are the minimum alternatives available to continue essential activities? What about costs, etc.? The SCM team will have to discuss this with the business managers and arrive at various risk-reduction measures, as well as recovery options, should the disaster occur. The discussion could result in buying one more purchase order system to be installed in a branch office as a disaster recovery back-up for the main system.

Implementation: Once the requirements have been finalised, it is necessary to implement the service continuity plans. These can range from keeping a few redundant machines, improved back-up procedures and awareness programmes, to a fully-fledged disaster recovery/business continuity site elsewhere. Implementation will involve detailed technical processes, testing and associated documentation.

Ongoing operational management: It is not enough to implement a service continuity plan and its associated activities as a one-off job. Service continuity management is a continuous task. It will involve IT services and the relevant departments in periodic awareness programmes, training, dry runs, testing and implementing additional services. If the organisation has implemented a standby purchase order system in a disaster recovery site, it must ensure that the back-up unit is kept in sync with the data and configuration of the main unit. If the main unit has been upgraded with a later version of the software and data, the SCM team should ensure that the back-up unit has the same version and data levels. Operational management will also involve dry runs, to test whether the back-up site can be used whenever necessary. The SCM team may make it mandatory for the purchase order team to visit the back-up site every month, to conduct a mock run on the back-up purchase order system. Conducting such dry runs will highlight several issues, deficiencies and requirements that need to be addressed if the organisation is to be satisfied with its disaster recovery site.

What is a business impact analysis?

A business impact analysis (BIA) is a detailed analysis of the effect on the business if a specific set of IT services is not available. It tries to determine the risks in terms of revenue loss, reputation loss and productivity loss, if the IT infrastructure, or other facilities, are down due to a disaster. A BIA will consider the following:

- Damage to premises and data centre.

- Damage to IT systems, such as servers, computers, networks and telecommunications.

- Damage to important data, in terms of loss or corruption.

- Loss of key staff, such as IT support, business managers and suppliers.

- Security threats, such as viruses or hackers who may steal confidential information.

- Damage and loss of power, air conditioners, etc. required for IT services.

- Damage due to sabotage, natural disasters, political threats and civil disturbances.

Each of the above should be considered in sufficient detail to ensure proper service continuity alternatives. Damage must be calculated in terms of revenue, reputation, security and employees. Based on the study, a detailed business continuity plan should be prepared and implemented to resume business processes following a disruption. Having a business continuity plan is a mandatory audit requirement for many reputable organisations. Organisations will not be able to generate business from other reputable organisations if they do not have a business continuity plan. For example, the RockSolid Corp may have to prove to its major external customers that it has adequate disaster recovery facilities and that RockSolid can provide essential services, even in the event of a disaster.

What options are available for service continuity?

Technically and financially it is possible to build a twin of an organisation. But not all organisations may want this, or can afford such a luxury. Service continuity is industry specific. The police, fire and ambulance services cannot afford to have their IT infrastructure down for even a few minutes.

Other organisations, such as a small automobile spare parts manufacturer, may be able to withstand an IT failure for a couple of days. Depending on the organisation, size, industry and budgets, companies can adopt a range of options:

- **Manual:** If it is possible, use manual methods.

- **Other offices:** If an organisation is decentralised and has many independent branches, then it may be possible to use the facilities in a working branch until the affected branch comes online again.

- **Cold standby:** Organisations can have an alternative site with basic computer and telecommunication facilities that can be switched on during extended failures.

- **Warm standby:** This involves re-establishing critical systems and services within a short period of time, usually achieved by having redundant equipment that can be used during disasters.

- **Hot standby:** This will involve having an alternative site with continuous mirroring of live data and configurations. This sort of facility is usually used by banks and the military, where it is not possible to have any downtime.

Who can invoke service continuity?

As part of their business continuity plans, organisations must first decide what qualifies as a disaster. Any routine equipment issues and maintenance downtime should not be termed a disaster, and alternative facilities invoked. Also, the decision to brand the current IT shutdown as a disaster must be taken only by senior business managers, in conjunction with senior IT managers. If the entire IT infrastructure is down due to a power fault, and is expected to be back up within a couple of hours, then organisations may not need to classify it as a disaster and start rushing employees to invoke their disaster recovery procedures. On the other hand, if it is sure that the power failure is more severe and may take an unacceptable time to restore, then the senior management may invoke disaster recovery procedures.

How can IT services be aware of risks?

In IT, risks are everywhere and at every step. Just because there have been no disasters in the past, does not mean there will be no disasters in the future. IT services must be constantly aware of how they handle their jobs and processes. A carelessly installed software patch may cripple an entire organisation. Every major incident or problem is a case study for risk and continuity management. IT services must constantly capture knowledge and best practices around risk identification and successful mitigation strategies. This can even be documented as a risk knowledge base. Risks can be gathered from a variety of internal and external sources. If there is a newspaper report of a new type of virus that has hit a certain organisation, then other organisations can immediately take precautions to see that the virus does not enter their premises.

In order to identify all possible risks and provide mitigation plans, organisations must first classify their entire IT infrastructure and services into categories of importance. Not all IT equipment in the organisation can be described as extremely important for the business. Businesses can categorise their entire IT services as being 'extremely important', 'important', of 'medium importance', or of 'low importance'. Some organisations call them Tier 1, Tier 2, etc. After undertaking a proper survey, the service continuity team can prepare a high-level table and start developing a mitigation plan for each classification.

Table 20 shows categories of importance, where Tier 1 is the most important.

Table 20: Categories of importance

Tier	Applications and services	Tolerable downtime	BCP plan	Remarks
1	Purchase System Finance servers Web server	Half a day	A1	
2	E-mail Sales servers	One day	B2	
3	Engineering	Two days	C4	
4	Other services	Five days	None	

What are the sub-processes of ITSCM?

ITSCM has the following sub-processes.

ITSCM support: This process makes sure that all members of IT staff with responsibilities for fighting disasters are aware of their exact duties, and that all relevant information is readily available when a disaster occurs.

Design services for continuity: This process is to design appropriate and cost-justifiable continuity mechanisms and procedures to meet the agreed business continuity targets. This includes the design of risk reduction measures and recovery plans.

ITSCM training and testing: This process is to make sure that all preventive measures and recovery mechanisms for the case of disaster events are subject to regular testing.

ITSCM review: This process is to review if disaster prevention measures are still in line with risk perceptions from the business side, and to verify if continuity measures and procedures are regularly maintained and tested.

CHAPTER 18: FINANCIAL MANAGEMENT FOR IT SERVICES

'When I had youth I had no money; now I have the money I have no time; and when I get the time, if I ever do, I shall have no health to enjoy life.'

Louisa May Alcott

What is IT financial management?

Financial management is the process of budgeting, accounting and charging for IT services. The objective of the IT financial management process is the proper management of monetary resources to support the organisation's IT goals. Financial management ensures that any solution proposed by IT services to meet the requirements defined in service level management, is justified from a cost and budget standpoint. Financial data provides the costs associated with the business to make decisions regarding changes in the IT infrastructure, systems, staffing or processes. If the business wants to add 100 more employees to the organisation, then IT financial management will provide all costs associated with the hardware, software, licensing and bandwidth required to add those 100 more users. Financial management is part of the service strategy phase of the ITSM core lifecycle.

The ITIL definition of financial management for IT services is:

'The function and processes responsible for managing an IT service provider's budgeting, accounting and charging requirements. Financial management for IT services secures an appropriate level of funding to design, develop and deliver services that meet the strategy of the organisation in a cost-effective manner.'

Why is financial management important?

Historically, IT has been viewed as merely a cost centre, or a luxury, in many organisations but in recent times businesses have realised the importance of having IT in their organisations. IT is also an expensive affair, and business managers and IT departments can disagree regarding the money constantly needed for infrastructure development. This is where IT financial management can help, by answering tough questions posed by business managers, finance departments and non-techies who approve and control most organisations' budgets. It can help in a better understanding of the costs of IT services. In most organisations the techies and IT services bear the brunt from business managers for frequent IT failures due to old and decaying IT equipment. However, the business managers will usually not approve new IT equipment unless they are convinced that it is necessary to spend a large sum of money for various upgrades. It is the responsibility of IT financial management to prepare a convincing proposal for necessary budgets that can get over the message '*spend money for IT stability or live with constant IT troubles*' to business managers.

Figure 15 illustrates the differences between having no financial management of IT and having an adequate system in place.

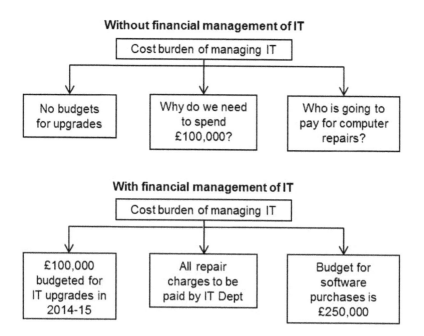

Figure 15: Inadequate and adequate financial management of IT

What are the responsibilities of IT financial management?

Some of the main responsibilities are:

- Budgeting

- IT accounting

- Charging

- Reports.

A fuller explanation of each is as follows:

Budgeting: Budgeting is the cost planning and predicting activity of the financial management process. When developing budgets, IT managers must plan for ongoing costs, future costs and upgrade costs of the various IT services. Budgeting will ensure that the actual spending can be compared with an accurate prediction, to prevent overspending, cover contingencies and plan for the future. Budgets and forecasts will have to be completed in discussion with business managers and agreed later and signed-off. Budgets can be completed for a year, or half-yearly, etc. The financial manager must gather information from a number of sources, including each department that uses IT services. It may be necessary to collect all IT costs associated with upgrading a software program on all the organisation's computers. The costs may include costs for purchase, implementation, maintenance and training. The IT department need not have a dedicated finance person for this. Any experienced IT manager, with some assistance from the regular finance department, can prepare a reasonably good IT budget.

Some of the common IT budgeting requirements will be for the following:

- Purchase of new computers, hardware, network equipment and software.
- Purchase of consumables – tapes, toner and disks.
- Annual maintenance charges for hardware and software.
- Payments to vendors and contractors.
- Payments for bandwidth usage and upgrades.
- Payments for IT repairs and replacements.
- Payments to telecommunications.
- Purchase of upgrades.

- Payments for ad hoc requirements.
- Total IT costs during initiation of new projects.

After studying all requirements, IT financial management can prepare a simple budget summary for the entire year and get it approved. Each type can have further sub details as required.

Table 21 shows a simple budget summary.

Table 21: A simple budget summary

Sl No.	Type	Approved budget
1	New computer, hardware and network item purchases	£100,000
2	New software purchases	£50,000
3	Telecom costs	£75,000
4	Consumables	£10,000
5	Annual maintenance costs	£25,000
6	Miscellaneous	£10,000

IT accounting: This involves monitoring the financial management process. It will involve proper accounting of the budget and how it is being spent (or recovered, if IT services are charging departments for their services). It involves preparing financial reports for management as the basis for future budgets. IT financial management may be asked to give a monthly breakdown of how the budget is being spent, so financial reports, such as the one shown in Table 22, may have to be prepared and presented to business managers. It is always best to liaise with your organisation's finance department to determine the kind of reports they would like to see.

Table 22: Monthly breakdown of budget

Budget for year 2014		Spend		
Type	Approved budget	Jan	Feb	Mar
New computer, hardware and network item purchases	100,000	17,000	12,000	25,000
New software purchases	50,000	5,000	8,000	2,000
Telecom costs	75,000	10,000	6,000	16,000
Consumables	10,000	1,000	1,000	2,000
Annual maintenance costs	25,000	3,000	1,000	5,000
Miscellaneous	10,000	800	1,200	300

By studying the IT accounting reports for a couple of years, the financial management team can predict, increase, or decrease amounts for future budgets.

Charging: In many organisations, IT services will charge end-users, and other departments, for IT services. The managers of the various business departments may be charged on a monthly, quarterly or yearly basis, for the various facilities and services they expect from IT services. IT services may charge a monthly fee of £50 for maintaining every computer used by the engineering department. In addition, there may also be costs for support requests after office hours and during weekends. Some departments may demand a higher level of service, or some other privilege from IT services. They may, therefore, have a different charging mechanism.

Some of the advantages of charging are:

- IT services will be able to earn revenue, and classify their services, resources and facilities accordingly.

- End-users and departments will have options to pay and demand better services.

- End-users and departments will understand that better services will involve higher costs.

Example: Charging a department for better services

Marketing Manager: 'Hello, tech manager. I demand your techies attend our computer troubles within an hour of calling.'

Tech Manager: 'Good morning. Our standard turnaround time is three hours free standard support. If you want it within an hour, it will be classified as priority support and we will charge £50 per incident that will be billed to your department. You okay with that?'

Marketing Manager: '£50? I think three-hour support is perfectly okay with us.'

Reports: Depending on the range of services provided by IT services, several types of report could be generated. Reports can be extracted from simple spreadsheets, or complex accounting software that can be linked to the budget.

Some tips and advice for financial management

- IT financial management teams must constantly liaise with several departments to understand current and future costs for hardware, software, telecom and services.

- Underpinning contracts must be periodically reviewed to understand current and future costs of a service or product.

- All unnecessary costs, such as maintenance agreements for unused equipment, must be stopped. Often much IT equipment cannot be used but payments could be happening via the finance department because nobody tells them to stop paying.

- Always have a strict control on 'nice to have' expenses, and concentrate on the 'must have' ones.

- Take a helicopter view of all the IT costs in every nook and corner of the organisation.

What are the sub-processes of financial management for IT services?

Financial management has the following sub-processes.

Financial management support: This process will define the necessary structures for the management of financial planning data and costs, as well as for the allocation of costs to services.

Financial planning: This process will determine the required financial resources over the next planning period (IT budget), and allocate those resources for optimum benefits.

Financial analysis and reporting: This process will analyse the structure of service provisioning cost and the profitability of services. The resulting financial analysis allows service portfolio management to make informed decisions when deciding about changes to the service portfolio.

Service invoicing: This involves issuing invoices for the provision of services and transmission of the invoice to the customer.

CHAPTER 19: SUPPLIER MANAGEMENT

'Quality in a product or service is not what the supplier puts in. It is what the customer gets out and is willing to pay for. A product is not quality because it is hard to make and costs a lot of money, as manufacturers typically believe. This is incompetence. Customers pay only for what is of use to them and gives them value. Nothing else constitutes quality.'

Peter F Drucker

Who is a supplier?

A supplier is a third-party organisation, or an individual, responsible for supplying goods and services. Examples are hardware and software vendors, networking and telecom suppliers, outsourcing companies and consultants. No organisation can do its business, or use IT, without depending on one or more suppliers, and suppliers have become important and critical business partners in most organisations worldwide.

Why are suppliers critical?

The main reasons why suppliers are necessary are as follows (the terms vendor and supplier are used interchangeably throughout this book):

- Organisations have become highly dependent on IT equipment, such as computers, laptops, servers, telecoms and networking. In many organisations, entire operations will be computerised and no alternate manual work is possible. Therefore, no organisation can survive without a competent and professional supplier supporting their IT infrastructure.

- Using IT equipment may be easy, but managing and supporting this equipment is a different ball game. It is not possible for an organisation's internal technical staff to have all the necessary knowledge to manage, troubleshoot and repair all equipment they use. This is because most IT equipment must be installed and configured only by the supplier, due to the technical knowledge, tools and expertise required. Also, only the supplier will have the spares and tools necessary to support the equipment during failures.

- The terms and conditions of an IT equipment sale by the supplier or manufacturer include terms and conditions related to warranty and support. IT personnel must adhere to these rules, in order that warranties remain valid and spares are provided. Fiddling with a piece of IT equipment without the necessary troubleshooting training, spares and tools can also be dangerous and destructive. It is not a simple task to rip open a hard disk to see if it can be repaired, without accepting the grave risk of losing all data and also permanently damaging the disk due to improper tools and handling methods. So organisations have to depend on suppliers for the necessary support.

- There could be a need for other kinds of assistance and support applicable to the industry and IT equipment being used.

What is supplier management?

In view of the preceding points, many organisations have dedicated supplier or vendor management departments.

Supplier management is a sub-process of the service design phase of the ITSM core lifecycle.

In a nutshell, supplier or vendor management will consist of the following high-level activities:

1. Identifying a set of qualified IT suppliers for your organisation.

2. Adding and removing suppliers.

3. Obtaining pricing quotes for equipment and services. Negotiating terms and conditions.

4. Implementing service contracts. Negotiating contracts with suppliers and managing them through their lifecycle.

5. Obtaining value for money from suppliers.

6. Managing relationships with vendors and suppliers.

7. Maintaining supplier policies.

8. Ensuring that underpinning contracts and agreements with suppliers are aligned with business needs.

9. Implementing best practices in supplier management.

Is it necessary to have contracts with suppliers?

It is absolutely necessary. If you are using external vendors to support or maintain critical equipment, or if you outsource some services, it is absolutely necessary to have a proper contract signed, and agreed, by both parties. The contract should be prepared in detail, covering the following:

- Scope of work
- Exclusions

- Roles and responsibilities
- Service hours
- Duration of contract
- Spares support
- Reports to be provided
- Payment terms
- Penalties for non-adherence.

Contracts should be prepared with the support of staff from technical, financial and legal departments, so that all aspects are properly covered and are worded accurately. A contract must withstand scrutiny by lawyers or the courts, if necessary. In addition, a detailed technical service level agreement (SLA) is also necessary to ensure proper support. Periodic audits should be conducted to see that SLAs are being met. Many companies think that by outsourcing work, they're ridding themselves of their internal responsibility. This is an incorrect assumption. Your organisation must also monitor the work, to ensure that it is progressing as expected. Even though you outsource the work, you can't completely outsource your responsibility to make sure everything is progressing smoothly. If all goes well with the outsourcer, you don't have much work to do. However, on many occasions the outsourcer may not perform to your expectations, and then you will have bigger issues. Remember that vendor problems eventually become your problem.

What are the key elements of a maintenance contract or a service agreement?

As mentioned before, it is necessary to have proper, written agreements with appropriate vendors, service providers and consultants that are responsible for maintaining critical services for an organisation. Without a clear, signed agreement, it is not possible to ensure, or expect, that the required assistance will be provided by external parties for essential activities in various situations.

A general purpose service agreement will normally cover the points listed below. Each point needs to be elaborated in clear and definitive terms for the area of coverage. Additional items can be added, depending on the specific nature of work or industry:

- Name of the project or area of support.

- Contract number or reference number, with date.

- Start date and end date for contract.

- Description of the project or work expected.

- Parties to the agreement, including authorised persons, departments and workplace addresses.

- Detailed scope of work.

- Common obligations of both parties.

- Out of scope (both parties).

- Assumptions, constraints, risks and limitations.

- Hardware, software, spares and other requirements.

- Legal aspects, jurisdiction and non-disclosure clauses.

- Financial aspects including budgets, payment terms, penalties, additional costs, extra charges, taxes and billing methods.

- Standard working hours or service windows covering number of hours per day and holidays.

- Number of staff required on site or on call.

- Training requirements.

- After-hours work, e.g. weekend work, if any.

- Help desk or support procedures, turnaround times for response, resolutions and workarounds.

- Incident and problem management procedures.

- Escalation procedures.

- Change management procedures.

- Reports and metrics (what standard reports will be exchanged).

- Project termination clauses, notice periods for closure.

- Signatures of authorised representatives from both parties.

Some tips and advice for supplier management

A very large percentage of organisations are not aware of the need, or advantages, of having a professional supplier or vendor management team within their organisations. However, implementing dedicated supplier management ensures organisations can get the best service and value from suppliers. Businesses expect quick and complete support from their suppliers. Without a professional supplier or vendor management team in your organisation, it is not possible to extract any meaningful, professional and responsive support from suppliers. It is not that all suppliers are slippery or unprofessional, but if you don't tell them what you expect of them, then they cannot help you. You need to tell them what service you need, how, when and at what cost, and then strike a balance, depending on your costs and limitations.

Some of the best practices for running a professional supplier management department are as follows:

- When buying goods and services from vendors, ensure you get all the correct commercial details, to avoid various hassles later. Typically, a commercial quote from a vendor should contain the following details:

  - Vendor letterhead with address and all contact details

  - Vendor tax numbers if applicable

  - Quote reference number and date

  - Attention: Purchaser's name and contact details

  - Validity of quote's expiration date

  - Item being sold and brief description

  - Unit price and currency

  - Quantity requested

  - Total cost

  - Applicable taxes and all other charges, such as insurance and freight

  - Shipping and billing address

  - Delivery period, if applicable

- Payment terms and conditions, such as advance payment and part payment, including bank or swift details if applicable for payments

- Warranty details, if applicable

- Signatures

- Vendor contracts, if any to be signed by the purchaser.

• For the equipment and service you buy, clearly articulate and document your priorities with a supplier. Without this, no vendor can do anything for you, however qualified they are. Once your requirements are clear, the vendor will be able to provide their requirements to meet your requirements.

• Create a competitive environment by having multiple vendors for the same product and service. This way you can negotiate good prices, speed and other value added services.

• Make use of the supplier's recommendations and white papers, these can help your business and prevent you from reinventing the wheel.

• Ensure the lowest price isn't the only aspect of supplier management. Other factors, such as their knowledge, the availability of qualified support staff, their name in the market and their client base, have to be considered. Many organisations haggle and argue based only on cost. For example, many companies compare a large conglomerate and a small shop selling a particular IT product, and demand discounts without understanding the scale, depth and overheads of each organisation.

This sort of comparison is inappropriate. You need to compare apples with apples only.

- Don't simply ditch a professional supplier when another supplier quotes 50p less. Often, many suppliers undercut costs just to clinch a deal and later recover those costs through other means.

- Be respectful to your suppliers and vendors. They are not pests. Don't be rude just because you can. If you have no intention of giving them business, don't simply invite them for empty discussions on pricing and services.

- Put everything in writing. Don't rely on verbal promises. Salespeople will promise you the world. Remember that if something is not in black and white, then it does not exist.

- Look at long term. Know your vendors strengths and weaknesses. Do some background research to assess their capabilities.

- Don't reveal one vendor's price to another. Many vendors can easily trick you into revealing prices. Be wary of such tactics.

- When buying products and services, don't pay for features you won't use.

- Get the right price. Not too low, not too high. Both have their disadvantages in the lifecycle of the product or service.

- The lowest price is not always the best price for the buyer. If your contract is not profitable to the suppliers, you won't get good service. In an outsourcing contract, the best staff of the outsourcing company will always be placed in the best-paying client's premises and not in the company that haggles over pennies.

- Don't accept gifts and other personal favours from vendors. Always maintain a professional distance.

- Unless the product or service is sold by no one else, always go for competitive bids, to ensure a good price. Always provide your requirements in writing and provide the same to each vendor, to avoid getting confusing quotes.

- Supplier management personnel should keep themselves abreast of new products and services in the markets, to know what vendors and suppliers are talking about. Subscribe to newsletters, attend seminars and visit websites that offer product comparison and articles about new products. You cannot be an IT supplier management executive or manager without the relevant IT knowledge to discuss products and services. A supplier management manager should be a 50% technical and 50% commercial person. He or she must be a technology guru with knowledge of hardware, software and systems, plus awareness of your business unit needs. They must also have other knowledge, such as negotiation skills, some experience in finance, legal aspects and documentation skills.

- Ensure adequate budgets for all purchases by discussing with the appropriate business managers.

- Implement vendor management tools and software to make your life easier. You can buy small to complex tools to raise purchase orders, manage contracts and manage inventory. Such tools can give you an easy view of all vendors, purchases till date and costs, and also generate reports for management. Manual methods become cumbersome over time.

- Be aware of your own limitations and constraints. Do not demand the sky when you are unable to pay for such services. Too many organisations demand top notch service from vendors, but have internal troubles, such as poor budgets, delays in payment and bureaucracy that prevents vendors from giving great service. Don't threaten or blackmail vendors. It ruins your reputation. Many organisations believe they can pressure vendors to give free and unrealistic services, but such practices backfire within a short time.

- When signing agreements, ensure you have them reviewed by your legal team to avoid the 'What the hell did you sign?' situation if something goes wrong later.

- Have a combination of small, medium and large suppliers. Do not buy small items from large vendors. The costs will invariably be high, as large vendors will have higher overheads.

- Be reasonable when demanding discounts. Suppliers respect companies that negotiate with them correctly. But many organisations make it a habit of demanding ludicrous discounts for every purchase because they believe they can bully vendors into offering a newer discount every week. It may work the first time, as vendors may cave in to clinch the deal, but once your organisation becomes known in the industry as someone who bargains hard, every vendor will jack their prices up by 30% and then create a drama of giving a 10% or 15% discount.

- Plan your purchases well so that you have time to negotiate effectively. Many organisations try to buy everything at the last minute, when internal deadlines and project pressures are high. If vendors get to know your urgency (and they most probably will), they will not be flexible and you will not get a good deal when you are under pressure.

- Know what you want and how much you are willing to pay. Do not be bowled over by flamboyant presentations and marketing gimmicks that try to justify a higher price.

- Learn to read the fine print in pricing quotes, contracts and value added extras. They can hold some really nasty surprises.

- When selecting vendors for critical equipment or services, ask lots of questions. It is also better to have more than one vendor for any product or service if possible. When one or more vendors go bust, you must be able to quickly locate another vendor, to maintain the service to your end-users. The questions you should ask for suppliers of critical services include: Does the vendor have enough trained support personnel to handle technical support? Does every support person carry a mobile, or a pager, for contact during emergencies or otherwise? Do they have adequate stock of critical spares? Do they have a 24/7 support option? Do they have a DR or BC plan? Can they provide references and/or any other testimonials or certification? Think of various ways in which that critical system can fail and ask the vendor how they can minimise that.

What are the sub-processes of supplier management?
Supplier management has the following sub-processes.

Providing the supplier management framework: This process provides guidance and standards for the procurement of services and products. This includes the provision of the supplier strategy and the preparation of standard terms and conditions.

Evaluation of new suppliers and contracts: This process evaluates prospective suppliers in accordance with the supplier strategy, and selects the most suitable supplier.

Establishing new suppliers and contracts: This process negotiates and signs a binding contract with a supplier. It is mainly applied for significant investments, either in externally provided services or in technology.

Processing of standard orders: This process orders for commodity products and services, and pre-defined items within the boundaries of existing contract frameworks.

Supplier and contract review: This process verifies if the contractually agreed performance is actually delivered, and defines improvement measures if required

Contract renewal or termination: This process will carry out regular renewals of contracts, to assess if those contracts are still relevant, and terminates contracts which are no longer needed.

CHAPTER 20: IT OPERATIONS MANAGEMENT FUNCTION

'The first rule of any technology used in a business is that automation applied to an efficient operation will magnify the efficiency. The second is that automation applied to an inefficient operation will magnify the inefficiency.'

Bill Gates

What is IT operations management?

This function focuses on the day-to-day, maintenance activities required to operate and support IT services. These operational actions involve executing repeatable, standardised procedures. They may also take assistance from other divisions and external vendors if required.

The ITIL definition of IT operations management is:

'The function within an IT service provider which performs the daily activities needed to manage IT services and the supporting IT infrastructure. IT operations management includes IT operations control and facilities management.'

What are the main responsibilities of IT operations management?

IT operations management conducts essential daily and routine activities required to monitor and control the health of the IT infrastructure, similar to periodic health check-ups for humans. Such day-to-day technical supervision and maintenance activities are required to maintain a stable and secure IT infrastructure. The activities performed by this group will include data back-ups, verification of back-ups and restores, print management, scheduling batch jobs, data centre maintenance, server room housekeeping, network cabling activities, database monitoring and storage monitoring. IT operations management will have standard operating procedures defined for a wide variety of their tasks and equipment.

Some best practices for IT operations

- **Adequate staffing:** Operational staff may not (or need not) be highly qualified staff. However, they must have the necessary training and competency to maintain IT equipment according to a given procedure. They need to diligently follow a set of steps, processes and procedures as prescribed by the manufacturer, or decided by the organisation. Also, there must be adequate staff to ensure a proper upkeep of all critical equipment. They should be provided with the necessary tools, training sessions, manuals, documents, spares and phones, to do their job. There have to be supervisory staff that will check on the operational staff to see if every activity assigned to them is being completed correctly.

- **Identify all equipment that needs maintenance:** All IT equipment and services that need maintenance or monitoring must be first identified for inclusion in operations. An organisation can have lots of IT equipment for differing services. Most of these will require periodic maintenance and monitoring, as prescribed by the manufacturer, to prevent overload, breakdown or other kinds of trouble. For example, a particular server may have to be kept within a prescribed temperature of 20°C or less, for it to function. Someone will have to regularly check whether the temperature is being maintained, or whether there are any system alarms that need attention. Or in another case, a disk space on a server may have to be monitored and usage limits enforced before it reaches critical stages.

- **Establish documents and procedures:** Most IT equipment needs maintenance exactly as prescribed by the manufacturer, for optimum functioning. Although there will be user manuals, it is better if you prepare customised documents and procedures to maintain the equipment. For example, you may use a heavy-duty printer in your company that needs periodic mechanical alignment to keep it working properly. Therefore, you may need to align the belt on the printer every fortnight, using the procedure prescribed by the manufacturer.

CHAPTER 21: GENERAL TIPS AND ADVICE FOR IT SERVICE MANAGEMENT

'The only thing to do with good advice is pass it on; it is never of any use to oneself.'

Oscar Wilde

Running and managing an IT department is not easy. It has its share of joys and woes, as it is highly exciting and also very stressful. You can have countless sleepless nights as you rush to your office in your pyjamas to revive a dead server. Many technical professionals and newcomers get pushed into managing an IT department, without enough training or experience and without a clear idea of what is expected of them. The troubles you could face can range from a constant stream of minor irritations, to absolute nightmares that could destroy you. IT management requires a greater mix of skills and expertise than any other business career. To be successful, you have to be a perpetual student, always learning something new. You need to: understand evolving technologies, master advanced business concepts, be a salesperson to sell IT to your management, manage complex projects, motivate technical staff (who are often more knowledgeable or intelligent than you!) and manage crisis after crisis. Not everyone can survive in this environment and the stress can lead to early burn-outs.

This chapter contains some general purpose tips and advice for running an efficient IT department. Some of the tips fall within the scope of ITIL, some may be outside this scope, while others fall in the grey area in-between. Some of the advice may seem short but separate departments or dedicated personnel to do the job are still required. The tips are not presented in any particular order:

- Learn language switching. That is, learn to talk technical with technical people and business with business people. Very often senior management may not understand your technology in detail but they need to know what the business impact of the technology is.

- Simplify your department. Whatever process or department you run, keep your structure simple and easy for others to understand.

- Minimise buzzwords and business jargon. A fancy name, such as strategic portfolio engagement services, does not really make sense to anyone, even if you try to explain.

- Understand the mantra of *'no knowledge, no management'*. Learn hands-on technical management. This means knowing how to install, operate, configure and undertake basic troubleshooting of all the IT equipment you have. Although you don't need to master every task, your team members do, so you should thoroughly understand your staff's work. Familiarise yourself with each person's responsibilities. Teach them and learn from them.

- IT is a constantly changing field, and you need to learn every day about new technologies and occurrences in the industry. Learning is not just enjoyable, but absolutely necessary to do the best job possible. Ensure adequate budgets for training and development, and encourage staff to participate in seminars, sales presentations and technical events, whenever possible.

- All IT managers must understand the business they support, and use this knowledge to build services and infrastructure that support business goals. You should also teach your direct staff how their work affects overall business goals. Publish your department's activities through status reports, regular communications and frequent project updates.

- Ensure you always have an accurate daily data back-up of all important servers. Restore periodically to verify. If possible, have the same kind of tape drives on all servers, to ensure compatibility of tapes and data restores from another if one drive fails.

- Ensure your organisation is fully compliant with software licensing. Software licensing is very important and you should have dedicated staff who can manage it on a day-to-day basis. Do not allow end-users to install whatever software and tools they want. Route them to a software asset management division.

- Periodically eliminate all unused hardware, software and other IT equipment.

- Have a good library of books relating to IT support, technical manuals, stress management and general management in your department. Do not have too many books of a similar nature or the same subject. Just one or two good books on each subject are enough to get good advice. Subscribe to magazines that are applicable to your department.

- Install a good help desk software package to manage your day-to-day support issues. Help desk software can provide multiple functionalities inside one package (purchasing, inventory, help desk, library and reporting) that can meet nearly 90% of a technical department's needs.

- Manage all IT assets properly. Asset management is a full-time critical function. Label all IT equipment clearly. Put stickers on all equipment, mentioning the purchase details, IP address, support numbers and asset tags. Maintain all equipment in its invoiced condition, for easy movement and disposal. Do not interchange equipment from different vendors or brands.

- Have CD-ROMs of all important software and tools, along with their licence keys and documentation, in a fireproof safe. In addition, have the contents loaded on a server for daily use whenever necessary.

- Have a private technical lab where your team members can experiment and play around with settings, install software and do some release and deployment.

- Have a proper storeroom to hold all your inventory of computers, software and other equipment. Monitor and control the movements properly. Get rid of all obsolete equipment as soon as possible.

- Ensure your team members get appropriate technical certifications. Put into place some safeguards to ensure they do not run away, or get snatched by the competition, immediately after getting heavily certified.

- Educate end-users on handling small support issues themselves. Install a small intranet to display FAQs for access by everyone. These can be steps for configuring printers, mail profiles, changing passwords and updating anti-virus programs. Periodically send e-mail tips to all end-users whenever you update the intranet, or need to send some technical advice to everyone.

- Ensure every system is properly patched with anti-virus updates as soon as the manufacturer releases them.

- Go around the offices to talk to end-users and understand their troubles and issues. You will gain a first-hand picture of what kind of issues end-users have.

- Have an emergency super-user or administrator password for every server, piece of network equipment and all other hardware or software that needs a password, and store them in a fireproof safe, accessible only to authorised personnel. In case of a trouble with the regular password or some other issue, the emergency passwords can be used.

- End-user education is very important to reduce your IT department's workload. Distribute a booklet or a pdf file of some essential dos and don'ts to every employee in your office.

- Ensure end-users do not store important data on their local drives. In case of a disk crash, you will not be able to help them.

- Have a corporate credit card handy to purchase several low-cost useful tools and utilities available on technical websites. Many tools and utilities are available for less than £20 and can be of immense help in many administrative and automation activities.

- Use old servers for archival purposes. You can connect old servers on the network to store old e-mails, instead of storing them on the local drives. Have a periodic back-up of the server.

- Ensure all hardware is patched regularly with bios, driver and firmware updates. These updates are released by the respective manufacturers and can solve many existing or future hardware troubles. You can reduce support issues and troubles if you keep your systems properly patched.

- Have all critical hardware and software under proper maintenance contracts.

- Protecting data is of paramount importance to any IT department. If you lose important data, all the hard work and the reputation you may have gained over the years, will go down the drain in an instant. Ask yourself the following questions to ensure proper disaster recovery:

  - Are you sure that you are backing up all important data every day?

  - Have your insured and properly labelled all equipment?

  - Are you sure that laptops do not contain sensitive information?

  - Have you ever tested the restoration of important data?

  - Is there any obsolete, outdated equipment or software you are still using which is not supported by vendors?

  - Do you have sufficient redundancy on your telephone and other communication links?

  - Are you following software-licensing guidelines properly?

- Is access to the data centre secure and for authorised persons only?

- Have you ensured that there is no electrical overload anywhere?

- Are all your critical and sensitive passwords secured?

- Are you sure that no unauthorised persons are accessing your network?

- Is your website safe from hackers?

- Are your employees writing their passwords on whiteboards provided to them?

- Do you have a proper firewall between your internal and external networks?

- Do you have spare and redundant power supplies on critical IT equipment?

- Are you adequately protected against spammers, hackers and other attacks?

- Are your senior management committed to spending enough on disaster recovery?

- Are your networks hacker proof?

- Do you have proper anti-virus protection?

- Is all your equipment labelled properly?

- Do you have fireproof safes to store back-up tapes and important documents?

- Do you have an off-site store for important documents and tapes?

- Is there a proper change management board to approve all technical changes to the infrastructure?

- Are there enough static eliminators in fire hazard areas and data centres?

- Is your electrical system and wiring of the proper standard?

- Do you have proper UPS and electric generators to handle long power outages?

• Have industry standard policies for all IT equipment usage and security. Some of the common policies you should have are:

- User ID, password and rights policy

- Anti-virus policy

- Asset disposal policy

- End-user back-up policy

- Server back-up policy

- Telephone usage policy

- Change management policy

- Copyright policy

- E-mail acceptable use policy

- E-mail archiving policy

- E-mail communications policy

- Equipment loan policy

- Firewall policy

- Instant messenger policy
- Internet usage policy
- Printer policy
- Purchasing policy
- Remote access policy
- Server space usage policy
- Software acceptance policy
- Software development policy
- Software installs policy
- Technology standards policy
- Telecommuting policy
- Third-party access policy
- Wireless access policy.

Other policies can be prepared depending on the need and nature of an organisation. You can also buy ready-made policies and modify them to your company's needs.

- Less is more. Reduce the amount of IT equipment and differing models you need to support. Standardise the hardware models, brands and software versions wherever possible. Install the same operating system build and the same versions of common applications on each desktop.

Finally, we can conclude this book with a small story about how IT departments should always be proactive to ensure peace of mind for themselves and their business.

The farmhand

A young man applied for a job as a farmhand. When the farmer asked for his qualifications, he said, 'I can sleep when the wind blows'. This puzzled the farmer, but he liked the young man and hired him nonetheless. A few days later, the farmer and his wife were awoken in the night by a violent storm. They quickly began to check things out to see if all was secure. They found that the shutters of the farmhouse had been securely fastened. A good supply of logs had been set next to the fireplace, and the young man slept soundly. The farmer and his wife then inspected their property. They found that the farm tools had been placed in the storage shed, safe from the elements. The tractor had been moved into the garage. The harvest was already inside. There was drinking water in the kitchen. The barn was properly locked. Even the animals were calm. All was well. It was only then that the farmer understood the meaning of the young man's words, 'I can sleep when the wind blows'. Since the farmhand did his work loyally and faithfully when the skies were clear, he was prepared for the storm when it broke. And when the wind blew, he was not afraid. He could sleep in peace. And, indeed, he was sleeping in peace.

Moral of the story?

There was nothing dramatic or sensational in the young farmhand's preparations. He just faithfully did what was needed each day. The story illustrates a principle that is often overlooked about being prepared for various events that occur in life. It is only when we are facing the bad weather that we wish we had taken care of certain things that needed attention much earlier.

APPENDIX 1: SAMPLE SLA BETWEEN IT SERVICES AND ROCKSOLID BUSINESS MANAGERS

Introduction

This service level agreement is a formalised and negotiated document between Technical Services Division and its customers, namely the end-users and business managers of RockSolid Corp. This document outlines the roles and responsibilities of both parties.

Suggestions for improvement, mistakes noticed and discrepancies in this document can be addressed to Mr James on 887879.

Agreeing parties

The agreeing parties are as follows:

- The Technical Services Division, also called IT Services, represented by its IT Managers.

- The Business, represented by the Business Managers.

Period

This SLA will be valid for one year from the date of signature by both parties, with an informal review every three months.

Reports

The IT Managers will generate agreed reports and send them to the Business Manager during the first week of every month.

Definition of IT support

The IT Service Desk has been set up to provide a single point of contact for RockSolid end-users to contact IT Services for any assistance. IT Services consists of several departments and employees. However, end-users can get all required IT assistance by contacting the Service Desk only.

Availability summary

The target availability for all RockSolid's IT services for end-users will be from 8 am to 8 pm on all business days. All maintenance activities will be done after business hours or at weekends, except for emergencies and unavoidable equipment failures.

Responsibilities of IT Services

IT Services is responsible for the following services to RockSolid end-users (this is also known as the service catalogue):

- All servers and data housed inside the Data Centre.

- All desktop computers, approved applications, printers and scanners installed in various departments of RockSolid Corp.

- All network equipment, such as routers, LAN switches, modems and other cabling.

- Providing Service Desk facilities to all end-users.

- A daily, full data back-up of all servers housed inside the Data Centre.

- The maintenance of access and security privileges – logon IDs, e-mail IDs and access to various servers.

- The provision of necessary software to end-users.

- The monitoring of the equipment.

- The provision of appropriate advice on upgrade requirements.

- Initiating emergency measures, if necessary.

- Maintaining, auditing and upgrading systems software.

- Vendor liaison for solving equipment issues.

- IT disaster recovery planning, testing and end-to-end management of disaster recovery.

- Maintaining an up-to-date inventory of equipment in production.

- Reviewing and updating this document periodically and publishing it on the RockSolid intranet.

- Anti-virus updates.

Responsibilities of the end-users and business managers

- Provide adequate forecasts on business volumes, new requirements and increase in employees.

- Release appropriate funds for necessary upgrades, new IT equipment and software licensing.

- Ensure any IT equipment is not misused, abused or experimented upon without a clear understanding of the consequences. Do not test freeware, shareware and hacking tools on the RockSolid network.

- Involve IT Services in all IT aspects related to various projects, capacity planning and new requirements.

- Make staff available to provide the necessary information, documentation and assistance to IT Services resource(s) with regards to resolving support issues.

- Accept and approve recommendations and costs put forward by IT Services from time to time on various support issues. Factor nominal infrastructure downtime in project planning and estimation.

- Do not prevent IT Services from fulfilling their obligations.

- Do not bring, install or use personal equipment and software (non-RockSolid owned) within RockSolid premises.

Exclusions

IT Services will *not* be responsible for:

- Loading paper to printers, or cleaning IT systems.

- Electrical systems maintenance.

- Ensuring back-up of data or files stored on local drives and test servers, unless specifically requested.

- Providing support or maintenance for obsolete and/or non-standard equipment, or for home PCs.

- Committing 100% service availability for any system or service.

- Providing support or assistance during civil disturbances, war, earthquakes, floods, curfews, terrorist attacks, bomb attack and other extraordinary situations.

Service desk hours

Technical assistance is available Monday to Friday, from 8 am to 8 pm, RockSolid business days.

Response

The standard turnaround time for all incidents will be three hours from time of call. Resolution of the issue may take more time depending on the type of incident.

Contacting the service desk

The IT service desk can be reached using any of the following methods:

- Phone number: dial 500 from any telephone.
- Service window: 8 am to 8 pm, Monday to Friday, RockSolid business days.
- E-mail address: *servicedesk@rocksolid.com*.
- All support requests must be in writing, with a description of the nature of the issue or request.
- Support calls will normally be attended on a first-come, first-served basis.
- Priority will be given to calls that disrupt business.
- After hours and weekend support currently *not* available.

Call resolution process

Should the users recognise a fault or incident with any service, a call should be placed with IT Services, providing information, such as business function affected and number of end-users affected, for assessment of severity. Depending on the nature of the call, appropriate action will be initiated.

All calls will be given an identification number. Hardware faults will need vendor interaction. Calls will be attended on a first-come, first-served basis. Priority will be given for calls that disrupt business and production servers.

Issues and limitations

- Non-availability of redundant or standby equipment for all services. 100% redundancy and standby equipment is not maintained for all equipment and services.

- Limitations on the number of IT support staff available for the number of end-users and equipment to support.

- Ad hoc major hardware and software requests to IT Services.

- External agencies and vendors not available on 24/7 support or after hours. Turnaround and resolution time may not be met in the event of major issues involving all IT Services members.

Unpredictable failures

Given the inherent complexities of RockSolid's IT environment and our reliance on external service suppliers, IT Services will take reasonable steps to protect the integrity of RockSolid's IT environment, but cannot guarantee that outages will never occur. IT Services can attempt recovery of systems and/or data only after the vendor restores system functionality in the event of hardware issues. Systems can fail during or after office hours. Recovery costs could be involved. IT Services will *not* commit 100% service availability for any system or service, nor guarantee that every incident or issue reported will have an immediate solution.

Appendix 1: Sample SLA between IT Services and RockSolid Business Managers

Equipment maintenance

IT Services is the owner of all computers, software and network equipment in RockSolid. Equipment will require periodic maintenance and upgrades to function at full capacity. IT Services will have windows for maintenance which will usually be after hours and at weekends. All major maintenance activities will be notified in advance and will not be classified as downtime.

Escalation procedures

End-users can use the following contacts for escalation if necessary:

Level	Name	Phone
First	Mr Richards	333
Second	Mr James	444
Third	Mr Jones	555

Signatures

IT Services Managers   Business Managers

APPENDIX 2: SAMPLE OLA BETWEEN IT DEPARTMENT AND THE ELECTRICAL DEPARTMENT

Agreeing parties

The IT Department represented by the IT Manager.

and

The Electrical Department represented by the Electrical Manager.

Scope

The Electrical Department agrees to provide the following services to IT Services:

- 24/7 UPS electrical power to all data centres and other areas connected by computers and associated equipment.

- All power supply faults to be attended within 30 minutes of reporting.

- Standby power to be supplied only to data centres in the event of extended outages.

- Routine electrical maintenance will be carried out once every three months on all power equipment, by giving advance notice to IT Services.

Signatures

IT Services Manager   Electrical Manager

APPENDIX 3: SAMPLE UC BETWEEN ROCKSOLID IT SERVICES AND ABC COMPUTER CORP

Agreeing parties

RockSolid IT Services represented by the IT Manager.

and

ABC Computer Corp represented by the Account Manager.

Scope

The ABC Computer Corp agrees to provide the following services to the IT Department of RockSolid Corp:

- Attend all calls within half a business day of reporting.

- Free replacement for all failed hardware items under warranty or maintenance contract within one business day of fault confirmation.

- 24/7 support for technical and hardware assistance to all mainframes installed in RockSolid Corp.

- Two ABC Computer Corp service personnel to be available on site, with pager and mobile access, between 9 am and 6 pm every business day.

- Monthly service reports to be provided by ABC Computer Corp to RockSolid Corp for release of payment.

Penalties

In the event that ABC Computer Corp fails to meet the above terms and conditions, RockSolid Corp reserves the right to impose penalties and deductions from monthly payments, including termination of contract, as agreed by ABC Computer Corp.

This contract is valid for one year, from January to December 2.

Signatures

RockSolid Corp   ABC Computer Corp

APPENDIX 4: A SIMPLE IT SERVICE MANAGEMENT FLOW WITH INTERACTIONS AMONG DIFFERENT PROCESSES

[Note: This is just a typical example. Responsibilities may overlap or be done together in various organisations.]

Example: Problem in a finance department

- All finance servers (CIs) freeze up every Monday. Need a reboot to begin work. Data often gets corrupted. Finance Department calls the Service Desk and logs the same request every Monday. Service Desk assigns call to Incident Management Team. Incident Management arrives and reboots the servers every Monday.

- Problem Management notices the trend and pattern of calls from Finance Department. Solution not available in known error database, hence it decides to investigate the problem. After investigation and research it concludes that it is necessary to upgrade to the new version of the payroll software to fix the problem. Initiates a request for change (RFC).

- RFC is sent to Change Management Team to upgrade all finance servers. CAB studies and approves the request.

- Capacity Management confirms that the finance servers have enough disk and memory to handle the new upgrade. No hardware purchases are necessary.

- Financial Management confirms availability of budgets for purchase of upgrade. Prepares proposal for purchase of software upgrade and gets it approved by business managers. Vendor supplies upgrade software in a few days.

- Release Management takes custody of software. It later tests the software in a test lab and prepares a build for easy deployment on all servers.

- Configuration Management Team provides current baseline for all finance servers from the CMDB.

- Deployment Management team takes a back-up of current baseline and installs the upgrade successfully.

- Immediately, Configuration Management and Release Management Teams together update the CMDB with details of the upgrade on the various CIs.

- Problem gets fixed. Servers do not freeze now. Solution entered in known error database by Problem Management for future reference.

APPENDIX 5: THE ITIL GLOSSARY

The official ITIL glossary can be obtained from the following websites:

www.itil-officialsite.com/InternationalActivities/ITILGlossaries_2.aspx

www.best-management-practice.com/knowledge-centre/news/itil-news/?di=588011.

APPENDIX 6: ITSM BOOKS AND OTHER RESOURCES

This concise guide has provided readers with the fundamentals of ITIL 2011 and its implementation. Readers interested in learning more in depth details on this subject should purchase the official ITIL Lifecycle Publication Suite.

All these books can be purchased directly from IT Governance Ltd:

www.itgovernance.co.uk/itil.aspx.

ITG RESOURCES

IT Governance Ltd. sources, creates and delivers products and services to meet the real-world, evolving IT governance needs of today's organisations, directors, managers and practitioners.

The ITG website (*www.itgovernance.co.uk*) is the international one-stop-shop for corporate and IT governance information, advice, guidance, books, tools, training and consultancy.

www.itgovernance.co.uk/itsm.aspx is the information page on our website for ITSM resources.

Other Websites

Books and tools published by IT Governance Publishing (ITGP) are available from all business booksellers and are also immediately available from the following websites:

www.itgovernance.eu is our euro-denominated website which ships from Benelux and has a growing range of books in European languages other than English.

www.itgovernanceusa.com is a US$-based website that delivers the full range of IT Governance products to North America, and ships from within the continental US.

www.itgovernanceasia.com provides a selected range of ITGP products specifically for customers in the Indian sub-continent.

www.itgovernance.asia delivers the full range of ITGP publications, serving countries across Asia Pacific. Shipping from Hong Kong, US dollars, Singapore dollars, Hong Kong dollars, New Zealand dollars and Thai baht are all accepted through the website.

Toolkits

ITG's unique range of toolkits includes the IT Governance Framework Toolkit, which contains all the tools and guidance that you will need in order to develop and implement an appropriate IT governance framework for your organisation. For a free paper on how to use the proprietary Calder-Moir IT Governance Framework, and for a free trial version of the toolkit, see *www.itgovernance.co.uk/calder_moir.aspx*.

There is also a wide range of toolkits to simplify implementation of management systems, such as an ISO/IEC 27001 ISMS or an ISO/IEC 22301 BCMS, and these can all be viewed and purchased online at *www.itgovernance.co.uk*.

Training Services

IT Governance offers an extensive portfolio of training courses designed to educate information security, IT governance, risk management and compliance professionals. Our classroom and online training programmes will help you develop the skills required to deliver best practice and compliance to your organisation. They will also enhance your career by providing you with industry standard certifications and increased peer recognition. Our range of courses offers a structured learning path from foundation to advanced level in the key topics of information security, IT governance, business continuity and service management.

ISO/IEC 20000 is the first International Standard for IT service management and has been developed to reflect the best practice guidance contained within the ITIL framework. Our ISO20000 Foundation and Practitioner training courses are designed to provide delegates with a comprehensive introduction and guide to the implementation of an ISO20000 management system and an industry recognised qualification awarded by APMG International.

We have a unique ITIL® Foundation (2 Day) training course designed to provide delegates with the knowledge and skills required to pass the EXIN ITIL Foundation examination at the very first attempt. This classroom course has been specifically designed to ensure delegates acquire the ITIL Foundation certificate in a low-cost, time-efficient way.

Full details of all IT Governance training courses can be found at: *www.itgovernance.co.uk/training.aspx*.

Professional Services and Consultancy

Our expert ITIL/ISO20000 consultants can help you to understand and manage the relationships between the service management processes and functions, showing how best to create an ITSM environment where processes are properly assessed, managed and continually improved to deliver value.

Using a 'forest' view of the service management processes, we can instil in you a clear understanding of how process output will impact the next process within the lifecycle of a service – and also the probable impact on each of the related processes. In this way, you can ensure that you control and manage so that poor service, unachieved goals and objectives, resource waste and many other risks do not arise in your organisation.

With IT Governance, all stakeholders can embrace the value of service management as described within the ITIL framework.

For more information about IT Governance Consultancy services, see: *www.itgovernance.co.uk/itsm-itil-iso20000-consultancy.aspx*.

Publishing Services

ITGP is the world's leading IT-GRC publishing imprint that is wholly owned by IT Governance Ltd.

With books and tools covering all IT governance, risk and compliance frameworks, we are the publisher of choice for authors and distributors alike, producing unique and practical publications of the highest quality, in the latest formats available, which readers will find invaluable.

www.itgovernancepublishing.co.uk is the website dedicated to ITGP enabling both current and future authors, distributors, readers and other interested parties, to have easier access to more information. This allows ITGP website visitors to keep up to date with the latest publications and news.

Newsletter

IT governance is one of the hottest topics in business today, not least because it is also the fastest moving.

You can stay up to date with the latest developments across the whole spectrum of IT governance subject matter, including: risk management, information security, ITIL and IT service management, project governance, compliance and so much more, by subscribing to ITG's core publications and topic alert emails.

Simply visit our subscription centre and select your preferences: *www.itgovernance.co.uk/newsletter.aspx*.

EU for product safety is Stephen Evans, The Mill Enterprise Hub, Stagreenan, Drogheda, Co. Louth, A92 CD3D, Ireland. (servicecentre@itgovernance.eu)

www.ingramcontent.com/pod-product-compliance
Lightning Source LLC
Chambersburg PA
CBHW071105050326
40690CB00008B/1123